LUKE

LUKE

The Gospel of the Son of Man

By

G. COLEMAN LUCK

MOODY PRESS

CHICAGO

Revised Edition 1970

ISBN: 0-8024-2042-7

10 11 12 Printing/LC/Year 87 86 85 84 83

Printed in the United States of America

CONTENTS

Introduction

THE PERFECT AND COMPLETE CHRIST is presented to man in each of the first four books of the New Testament. At the same time it is likewise true that each of these four writings emphasizes a slightly different aspect of His many-sided character. For hundreds of years, students of the Scriptures have observed that Matthew presents Jesus especially as the promised King of Israel; Mark calls attention to Him as the great Servant of Jehovah; Luke stresses His perfect manhood; while John brings to the forefront His deity.

It is surprising to note that the faces of the four cherubim (as described in Rev. 4:7 and Ezek. 1:5, 10) correspond to the emphases mentioned above. The lion, who is king of the beasts, suggests the gospel of Matthew. The calf (or ox), the plodding servant of man, reminds us of the gospel of Mark. The man speaks of course of the

7

gospel of Luke; and the flying eagle, soaring high into the heavens, is a fitting symbol of the gospel of John.[1]

These same four features are strikingly brought out by the great Old Testament Messianic prophecies which speak of Christ as the "Branch." "The Branch of David" (Isa. 11:1; Jer. 23:5; 33:15) is Matthew's picture of Christ. Mark tells of "my servant the BRANCH" (Zech. 3:8). Luke portrays "the man whose name is The BRANCH" (Zech. 6:12), while John presents "the branch of Jehovah" (Isa. 4:2, ASV).

THE PURPOSE OF LUKE

The first and most obvious purpose of Luke's gospel is a *historical* one: to present an accurate account of the facts about the life of Christ. "Forasmuch as many have taken in hand to draw up a narrative concerning those matters which have been fulfilled among us, even as they delivered them unto us, who from the beginning were eyewitnesses and ministers of the word, it seemed good to me also, having traced the course of all things accurately from the first, to write unto thee in order, most excellent Theophi-

---

[1]"The early Church saw this. And with one voice they testify to what they saw, namely, that the Four Gospels contained four different aspects of the Great Manifestation. And though to say that the Fathers so viewed the matter may not in these days commend the view, it will at least prove that the doctrine here is no novelty. The emblem which they applied to the Gospels was that of the Four Cherubim or 'living creatures,' conceiving that these four 'living creatures' were apt representations of the Four Evangelists or Gospels, or rather, more correctly to express their thought, of those manifestations of Christ Himself which the Four Gospels respectively present to us, Christ Himself being one and the same in each, yet seen and set forth by each in a different aspect" (Andrew Jukes, *Four Views of Christ,* p. 16).

lus; that thou mightest know the certainty concerning the things wherein thou wast instructed" (Luke 1:1-4, ASV).

In addition to this it is evident that the book has a *spiritual* purpose. The writer presents to our view Jesus Christ as the perfect God-Man, who after a perfect ministry provided perfect salvation for sinful humanity. In a remarkable way the book pictures the perfect Man as the Saviour of imperfect men. A key verse to the entire presentation is 19:10: "For the Son of man is come to seek and to save that which was lost."

Twenty-six times the key phrase "Son of man" is found in the gospel of Luke. This expression certainly emphasizes the humanity of Christ in contrast to the phrase "Son of God," which stresses His deity. But it does more than this. It means that He is the perfect, ideal Man, the true Representative of the whole human race. As such He is the One rightfully "anointed . . . with the oil of gladness above . . . [His] fellows" (Heb. 1:9), the true Messiah ("anointed One"). C. I. Scofield, in commenting on the same phrase as applied to Ezekiel, has cogently written,

As used of Ezekiel, the expression indicates, not what the prophet is in himself, but what he is to God: a son of man (a) chosen, (b) endued with the Spirit, and (c) sent of God. All this is true also of Christ who was, furthermore, the representative man—the head of regenerate humanity.[2]

---

[2]C. I. Scofield (ed.), *Scofield Reference Bible*, p. 842.

The key word of Luke's gospel is "save." Together with
the forms "Saviour" and "salvation," the word is used
twenty times in the book. In a nutshell, so to speak, it gives
the message of the gospel of Luke as a whole.

The third purpose for the writing of the book was a
personal one. Luke originally addressed his gospel to a
man named Theophilus which in Greek signifies either
"lover of God" or "loved by God." Theophilus was
apparently a high official of some sort, because the word
which is translated "most excellent" (1:3) is used elsewhere in the New Testament only of governors (Acts
23:26; 24:3; 26:25). The man was evidently a Greek
nobleman, but additional information about him is lack-
ing. Most important of all, he was a Christian, for Luke
writes to him so that he may "know the certainty of those
things, wherein thou hast been instructed" (1:4). The
book of Acts was addressed to this same person (Acts 1:1).
Since Acts was obviously written before the death of Paul,
which occurred about A. D. 68,[3] it seems reasonable to
conjecture that the gospel of Luke (which was completed
before Acts) must have been written around A. D. 60.

INTERESTING FEATURES OF THE
GOSPEL OF LUKE

More than half the material found in this gospel is not
in any of the other three. It has been said that if one
should arbitrarily consider the books as consisting of one
hundred parts, fifty-nine of these would be exclusive to

[3]*International Standard Bible Encyclopaedia*, IV, 2287.

Luke, and forty-one in one or more of the other gospels. This exclusive material includes nine miracles, thirteen parables, as well as various messages and events.

Luke in keeping with his purpose tells more of the birth of Christ than any other gospel, and he alone writes of the boyhood of Jesus. He alone recounts the birth of the forerunner, John the Baptist. He gives half a dozen details about the crucifixion not found elsewhere. Only Luke relates the resurrection appearances to Cleopas and to Peter, as well as other important details in connection with this great event.

Luke alone gives certain important dates. These are to be found in 1:5; 2:1; 3:2; 3:23.

Luke has been called "the Gospel of Womanhood" because of numerous references to women not to be found in the other gospels. These include Elizabeth (chap. 1), facts regarding Mary (chap. 1), Martha and Mary (10:38-42), the widow of Nain (7:12-15), women who ministered to Christ (8:2-3), the weeping women near the cross (23:27-31), the sinful woman (7:37-50).

Luke has also been called "the Universal Gospel" because of various references to Samaritans and Gentiles, because of the tracing of the lineage of Christ back to Adam (3:38), and because of the absence of Hebrew words such as are to be found in other gospels.

Luke covers a period of about thirty-five years in the events described. The story opens with the announcement to Zacharias of the birth of John the Baptist. It closes with the ascension of Christ after His death and resurrection.

THE HUMAN AUTHOR OF THE BOOK

As with the other gospels, the human writer of the book
never calls himself by name. He does, however, use the
first person singular pronoun in 1:3. From earliest times
Christians have considered the author to be Luke,[4] a close
friend and fellow worker of Paul. Some authorities believe
that because of his name, his profession, the type of Greek
he writes, and the person he addresses, Luke must have
been a Greek himself, a Gentile Christian.[5] If so, he is
the only Gentile writer in the entire Bible.

External evidence for Lukan authorship is convincing.
Beginning with Irenaeus, an outstanding Christian
teacher of the last half of the second century A. D., the early
church Fathers agree that Luke was the author of this third
gospel. Irenaeus was a student of Polycarp, Bishop of
Smyrna, who himself in his youthful days was a disciple of
the aged Apostle John. His testimony is therefore particularly valuable.

The internal evidence certainly harmonizes with this
church tradition. The writer of the third gospel was the
same as the author of Acts. Comparison of the opening
verses of each book proves this beyond question. The
writer of Acts was a companion and associate of the Apostle
Paul. This is verified by the well-known "we" sections of

[4]"The first writers who definitely name Luke as the author of the Third
Gospel belong to the end of the 2d cent. . . the ancients universally agreed
that Luke wrote the Third Gospel" (*Ibid.*, III, 1937) .

[5]"We may most surely conclude that Luke was a Gentile by birth—as the
author of Luke-Acts appears to have been, to judge by some internal
evidence" (E. K. Simpson and F. F. Bruce, *The New International Commentary on the New Testament: Ephesians and Colossians,* pp. 307-8) .

the Acts of the apostles. Three times the author of the book
abruptly ceases to tell of what "they" did and begins to say
"we" did so and so. These passages are 16:9-12;
20:5—21:18; 27:1—28:16. In each case the material in
question has to do with the travels of Paul. Significant
references in the Pauline Epistles prove that Luke was
indeed a frequent companion of Paul (Col. 4:10-14;
Philemon 24; II Tim. 4:11).

Greek authorities furthermore tell us that there are
numerous technical medical terms used by the author in
both Luke's gospel and the book of Acts.[6] Several samples
of this are: "taken" and "a great fever" (Luke 4:38); "full
of sores" (i.e., ulcerated), "in great pain" (16:20-25,
Today's English Version); "great drops" or clots of blood
(22:44). Since Luke was "the beloved physician" (Col.
4:14) it would have been natural for him to use such
terms.

---

[6]H. D. M. Spence, *Pulpit Commentary,* Vol. XVI, Part 2, p. xix.

Outline of the Book

I. THE ANNOUNCEMENT AND ADVENT OF THE SON OF MAN
   (1:1—4:13)
   A. His Birth and Childhood (1:1—2:52)
      1. Preface (1:1-4)
      2. Announcement of the Miraculous Birth of the
         Forerunner (1:5-25)
      3. Announcement of the Birth of Jesus to Mary
         (1:26-38)
      4. Mary Visits Her Cousin Elizabeth (1:39-56)
      5. Birth of John the Baptist (1:57-80)
      6. Birth of Jesus, the Son of Man (2:1-20)
      7. Circumcision of Jesus (2:21)
      8. Presentation of the Infant Jesus at the Temple
         (2:22-38)
      9. Boyhood of Jesus (2:39-52)
   B. The Preparation for His Ministry (3:1—4:13)
      1. Ministry of John the Baptist (3:1-20)
      2. Baptism of the Son of Man (3:21-22)
      3. Genealogy of the Son of Man (3:23-38)
      4. Temptation of the Son of Man (4:1-13)

16. He Casts the Demons out of the Man of Gadara (8:26-39)
17. He Heals the Woman with the Issue of Blood and Raises the Daughter of Jairus (8:40-56)
18. He Sends Forth the Apostles on a Preaching Tour (9:1-10)
19. He Miraculously Feeds Five Thousand (9:11-17)
20. He Receives Peter's Confession, Directly Announces His Death for the First Time, and Teaches the Method of True Discipleship (9:18-26)
21. He Is Transfigured on a Mountain (9:27-36)
22. He Relieves a Demon-possessed Child and Again Predicts His Death (9:37-45)
23. He Rebukes Pride and Bigotry (9:46-50)

B. His Ministry During the Last Journey to Jerusalem (9:51—19:27)
   1. He Begins the Journey to Jerusalem and Is Forced to Rebuke the Disciples on the Way (9:51-62)
   2. He Sends out Seventy Disciples as Forerunners on a Preaching Trip (10:1-24)
   3. He Gives, in Response to a Lawyer's Questions, the Parable of the Good Samaritan (10:25-37)
   4. He Visits Martha and Mary and Shows That Communion with Himself Is the One Absolutely Needful Thing (10:38-42)

IV. THE RESURRECTION AND ASCENSION OF THE SON OF MAN
   (24:1-53)
   A. He Rises from the Dead and Appears to the Disciples (24:1-49)
   B. He Ascends to Heaven and the Disciples Return to Jerusalem (24:50-53)

1

The Announcement and Advent
of the Son of Man

(1:1–4:13)

His Birth and Childhood (1:1–2:52)

Preface (1:1-4)

IN THESE INTRODUCTORY VERSES, Luke plainly declares his purpose. He indicates that many had undertaken to write in logical order the facts about the life of Christ. It should be observed that he separates himself from the apostles— the eyewitnesses: "even as they delivered them unto us, which from the beginning were eyewitnesses, and ministers of the word" (v. 2). The writer claims that he himself has "had perfect understanding of all things from the very first" (v. 3). The Greek expression translated "from the very first" could be rendered "from above" and some expositors understand it as being a direct claim to inspiration.[1] While this wonderful book was undoubtedly writ-

---

[1]E.g., C. I. Scofield (ed.), *Scofield Reference Bible,* p. 1070.

ten under the inspiration of the Holy Spirit, it is highly
questionable that Luke, at this point, is advancing such a
teaching. The same word *(anothen)* is also found in Acts
26:5 where it is evident that the translation "from the
beginning" is completely proper. The authorized translators are very likely correct here also in their rendering.
When Luke states that he has "traced the course of all
things accurately from the first" (ASV) he simply means
from the time that these momentous events began to
transpire. In the following verses he goes back farther than
do the other gospel writers, telling of the very first in the
chain of marvelous happenings which commenced the New
Testament period: the angelic announcement of the birth
of John the Baptist.

When Luke says that he has written "in order" (v. 3) he
does not mean that all the events he depicts are in exact
chronological order, but rather that everything is related
in an orderly and entirely accurate manner, in contrast to
the other somewhat confused accounts which he mentioned in verse 1.

*The Announcement of the Miraculous Birth of the Fore-
runner* (1:5-25)

After four brief verses of introduction, Luke presses
immediately into his thrilling narrative. Verses 5-7 contain
interesting facts concerning Zacharias and Elizabeth, the
parents of John the Baptist. Zacharias, we learn, was a
priest and "of the course of Abia" (see I Chron. 24:10).
King David had long before divided the priests into

twenty-four groups. Each group took its turn in officiating at the temple for a week at a time. This arrangement still prevailed in New Testament days. The wife of Zacharias, Elizabeth, was also a descendant of Aaron. This husband and wife were truly godly people and, as far as was humanly possible, they diligently kept the Old Testament law (v. 6). But, as experience has often proved, the children of God do not necessarily escape the trials and tribulations of this earthly life. This couple, like Abraham and Sarah of old, had grown to advanced age without having a child of their own. This was to them a great sorrow; much greater, no doubt, than it would be to a similar couple nowadays.

While officiating in the priestly office, Zacharias saw an angel (vv. 8-11). He was taking his turn at the temple service and was for the moment alone in the holy place, bringing the sacred incense before the Lord. This was done at both the time of the morning and evening sacrifices. Many people were standing outside in the court of the temple praying. Suddenly an angel appeared to the aged man.

The angel proceeded to give his divine announcement (vv. 13-17). Zacharias was troubled and afraid, as even the best men usually were in the presence of these supernatural beings. The angel, however, kindly encouraged him to "fear not." This was a tremendous moment. It was the first time in over four hundred years, as far as we know, that God had directly spoken to His people.

Zacharias had in earlier years prayed often for a son,

though evidently he had stopped such prayers long before this time. Now he learned at last that his petition had been heard. God in His own time and way always answers the prayer of faith. In this case Zacharias and Elizabeth would have a son, and this child was to be called by the name of John (meaning "the Lord is gracious"). John would bring joy and gladness to his parents and their friends. For the fulfillment of this, read verse 58. Furthermore this child would in later life be "great in the sight of the Lord" (1:15). This is indeed the only true greatness. John was to drink no wine nor strong drink. Apparently this meant he was to be a Nazarite from birth (cf. Num. 6:3). Only two others are said in the Bible to have been Nazarites from birth: Samson (Judges 13:7) and Samuel (I Sam. 1:11). Most wonderful of all, John would from the very beginning be filled with the Holy Spirit.

His eventual ministry was to be an ideal one—he would turn many Israelites to the Lord. He would go before the Lord and have the task of introducing people to Him. Although he would not actually be Elijah returned to earth again, he would perform his ministry "in the spirit and power of Elijah" (1:17a, ASV). His preaching would turn the hearts of careless parents to a real spiritual concern for their children. Also he would bring back the hearts of disobedient, rebellious children to "the wisdom of the just" (1:17b). He would "make ready a people prepared for the Lord" (1:17c). Oh, that each child of God might perform a similar service nowadays!

This good man, though possessing real faith in the Lord, still had considerable unbelief in his heart. Doubting the angelic announcement, he was stricken with dumbness (which lasted at least nine months) because of his sin (vv. 18-20). The mighty angel proclaimed himself to be Gabriel, the same one who many years before had brought to Daniel the prophecy of the seventy weeks (Dan. 9:21). No doubt, to the mind of Zacharias, there came the recollection of the way Daniel had received the messages of Gabriel in complete faith, in contrast to himself.

When Zacharias emerged, the people waiting outside for his benediction saw that he had had some unusual experience in the temple (vv. 21-25). Finishing the work assigned to him, he departed for his home. There, in accordance with the promise of the angel, Elizabeth became pregnant, and passed a period of five months in seclusion. At this point a second marvelous supernatural manifestation took place, happening this time to a cousin of Elizabeth—Mary of Nazareth.

Announcement of the Birth of Jesus to Mary (1:26-38)

Gabriel met Mary and saluted her (vv. 26-29). We should follow the example of the angel and not, on the one hand, glorify Mary nor, on the other hand, belittle her. When Gabriel called her "highly favoured," Roman Catholic translators render the expression "full of grace" and interpret the phrase to mean that Mary is "full of grace" which she can dispense to others. The American Standard Version margin, however, shows that the expression means "endued with grace," that is, graciously accepted, or much graced. The thought is that Mary was about to be *given* much grace, or unmerited favor, and thus would be "highly favored" or "full of grace."

The wonderful prophetic statements of verses 30-33 should be carefully observed. Of these seven prophecies the first five have long ago come to pass. These all have to do with Christ's first coming.

The last two predictions have to do with His second coming, and still remain to be fulfilled. Verse 31 took place at His first advent and is a fulfillment of Isaiah 7:14. Verse 32 has not yet been fulfilled. When it does take place in connection with the second advent, Isaiah 9:6-7 and a multitude of other kingdom prophecies of the Old Testament will be a reality.

Mary did not express any doubt, as did Zacharias, but simply asked frankly how all this was to take place in view of the fact that she had had no relationship with a man (vv. 34-38). The angel explained that the miracle would be wrought through the divine power of the Holy Spirit. The One born of her would be utterly and completely holy—the Son of God. Gabriel encouraged Mary by revealing to her God's miraculous working with her cousin Elizabeth. Verse 37 is a truly great statement: "For with God nothing shall be impossible." Mary meekly and submissively agreed to the Lord's will for her life, even though she must have realized that it would likely cause her embarrassment and misunderstanding.

Mary Visits Her Cousin Elizabeth (1:39-56)

Mary visited Elizabeth, and when she entered the room, Elizabeth was "filled with the Holy Ghost" (v. 41). It was divinely revealed to her that her cousin was to be "the mother of my Lord" (v. 43). Mary was pronounced as "blessed" (or, "happy") because of her faith in believing the Lord's promise.

Mary's expression of praise (vv. 46-56) has traditionally been called the Magnificat. Her words show a real acquaintance with the Old Testament Scriptures, especially with the book of Psalms and with the song of Hannah (I Sam. 2:1-10). It is significant to observe that she talked of "my Saviour" (v. 47) and of her "low estate" (v. 48) but gave not the slightest hint of any "immaculate conception" for herself or of her "sinlessness" which Rome today claims for her.

Birth of John the Baptist (1:57-80)

John was born, circumcised and named (vv. 57-66). The fact that the people "made signs" to Zacharias (v. 62) indicates that he must have been deaf as well as dumb, as a punishment for his unbelief.

When his mouth was finally opened, he uttered a truly wonderful statement of praise (vv. 67-79), sometimes called the Benedictus, from the opening word in the Latin version. As a prophet, he spoke of God's redemption as though it were already complete. Remarkable insight was shown as to the future ministry of both John and Christ.

Even as in Gabriel's announcement to Mary, truths concerning both the first and second comings of our Lord were brought together. "The dayspring" (v. 78) is Christ Himself. Zacharias mentions the incarnation (vv. 69, 78), the blessed life of the saved ones (vv. 74-75), the work of John (v. 76) and the ministry of Jesus (vv. 69, 79).

The Birth of Jesus, the Son of Man (2:1-20)

The expression "in those days" (v. 1) is, indeed, significant.

At the time Augustus issued his momentous decree, the doors of the temple Janus in Rome had been closed for a decade and were to remain closed for some thirty years longer. This signified that there was peace throughout the Empire. When Rome was at war these doors were thrown open. What was once the Roman Republic had now been succeeded by the Roman Empire. A single autocratic ruler now controlled the Mediterranean world. The peace which existed was the Pax Romana—the peace of the mailed fist. "In those days" the Prince of peace came to this earth!

In words very pertinent to our own day, G. Campbell Morgan writes:

> That was the most damnable condition the world had ever seen. I am not glorifying war; but when the reason of no war was that the people were bludgeoned into submission, so that no man or woman, boy or girl dare peep, or chirp or mutter, or call his soul his own, or her own,

because of the despot on the throne; that was the darkest hour the world has ever seen.[2]

The supreme potentate was Caesar Augustus, formerly known as Octavius, the grandnephew of Julius Caesar, and the first of the Roman emperors. From him went forth the order that "all the world should be taxed," or better, "enrolled" (ASV). Doubtless the enrollment was for the eventual purpose of taxation. This was a most unusual and troublesome decree. Of what concern was it to Caesar that millions of little people, among them Joseph and Mary, were inconvenienced? No doubt the emperor had what he considered to be sufficient reasons for his command. However, he little knew or cared that he was actually causing to be fulfilled the divine prophecy of Micah 5:2: "But thou, Bethlehem Ephratah, though thou be little among the thousands of Judah, yet out of thee shall he come forth unto me that is to be ruler in Israel; whose goings forth have been from of old, from everlasting" (cf. Matt. 2:4-6). In that day it appeared that Augustus was a most important person—millions moved at his beck and call. Joseph and Mary were just humble and insignificant people. Yet it can now be easily seen that Caesar was the really insignificant person—merely a pawn in the plan of God. Joseph and Mary were by far the most important persons on the face of the earth at that particular moment because Mary had within her womb the Saviour of the world.

---

2 G. Campbell Morgan, *The Gospel According to Luke,* pp. 34-35.

At the very time Joseph and Mary were present in
Bethlehem, the hour of birth came. The Messiah was born,
not in a palace, but in a stable because "there was no room
for them in the inn" (v. 7). Following the birth of Christ,
the great Shepherd (Heb. 13:20), the first announcement
was made by angels to humble human shepherds (vv. 8-
10). They were told that unto them was "born . . . a
Saviour" (v. 11). Though the world little realizes it, this is
what it needs more than anything else—a Saviour. This
Saviour was the Christ—the promised Messiah of the Old
Testament. He was also the Lord, the Word who "was
God" and who "became flesh" (John 1:1, 14, ASV). In the
angel's expression of praise (Luke 2:14), "in the highest"
refers not to the highest degree but to the highest realm,
heaven itself. In heaven there is glory to God; on earth
there is to be peace. This peace is realized by those who
receive God's Son: "Therefore being justified by faith, we
have peace with God through our Lord Jesus Christ"
(Rom. 5:1). In Christ, God the Father magnifies His all-
surpassing "good will toward men." "For God so loved the
world, that he gave his only begotten Son" (John 3:16).

As soon as they heard the announcement, the shepherds
dropped everything in order to go to Bethlehem (vv. 15-
16). There they had the joy of seeing the Christ Child.
Many others also learned of this wonderful event, for the
shepherds spread the tale far and wide (v. 17). But with
the passing of years, the story grew dim in the minds of
men. Mary, however, did not forget (vv. 18-19).

The Circumcision of Jesus (2:21)

By this rite the true humanity of Jesus is further revealed. All was accomplished according to the law of Moses (Lev. 12:3). The name commanded by the angel was then officially given to the Infant.

Presentation of the Infant Jesus at the Temple (2:22-38)

The firstborn child, according to the law (Exodus 13:2; Num. 8:17), had to be particularly presented to the Lord. It is significant that Joseph and Mary brought the sacrifice which was especially prescribed for the poor (cf. Lev. 12:2-8).

Verses 25-35 contain the worship and prophecy of Simeon, a godly old man who was expectantly waiting for the Messiah. It may perhaps be that through study of the "Seventy Weeks" prophecy of Daniel 9, Simeon realized that the time was near. The Holy Spirit (notice this instance of His pre-Pentecost ministry) revealed to this aged saint the fact that he would see the Messiah before he died. So he was waiting for "the consolation of Israel" (v. 25b) —Christ Himself. Spirit-guided he was shown that this Babe was the One whom he sought. He then announced himself quite ready to leave this earthly sphere now that he had seen "thy salvation." To see Jesus Christ is to see God's salvation. Simeon prophesied that this child would some day "lighten the Gentiles" (v. 32a). After this He would be "the glory of thy people Israel" (v. 32b). Jesus is the true glory of the nation Israel. Sad to say, they do not as a nation realize this now, but someday they will. Because of the Lord Jesus many in Israel will "fall" (v. 34). But, happily, some will "rise again." Of this, Saul of Tarsus is an outstanding example. He first stumbled at the Messiah, but later rose again to be a flaming evangel. During the two millenniums that have intervened, many other Israelites have become active and useful Christians.

The parenthetical expression "Yea, a sword shall pierce through thy own soul also" (v. 35) is addressed directly to Mary and is undoubtedly a prediction of the suffering of mind she would undergo when she saw her Son crucified at Calvary. That she was personally present when that tragic event took place, we know of a surety (John 19:25).

Verses 36-38 record the praises of Anna, a godly woman who is termed a "prophetess." This does not necessarily mean that she foretold the future but rather indicates that she was a teacher of the Word of God. Considering twelve to have been the youngest age at which she could possibly have been married, she must at the time of the presentation have been at least one hundred and three years old, for she had been a wife for seven years and a widow for eighty-four years. It is said that this aged saint "departed not from the temple" (v. 37). Evidently some small chamber in the temple confines had been made available for her use as living quarters. Though the infirmities of age prevented her from carrying on a public ministry, she still "served God with fastings and prayers night and day."

Her example should be an encouragement to those in a like condition.

Anna, as well as Simeon, was privileged to see the Christ Child. Like him, she "gave thanks" to the Lord for His great mercy. Later she told other pious people of Jerusalem—those who "looked for redemption"—about the Saviour upon whom she had gazed.

The Boyhood of Jesus (2:39-52)

Once again the complete humanity of Jesus is shown. Yet at the same time He appears, even at the age of twelve, as more than a man. Verses 39-40 summarize the opening twelve years of His life on earth. During this time He lived at Nazareth, a city which for reasons now obscure seems to have sustained a bad reputation in that day. The statement of verse 40 that "the child grew, and waxed strong in spirit, filled with wisdom: and the grace of God was upon him" refers of course to His humanity, not to His deity. That Christ possessed both a divine and a human nature, the New Testament makes abundantly clear. The exact relationship between these two natures is not, however, revealed to us. Doubtless we will do well to emulate this discreet silence of Scripture. It can certainly be stated with confidence that at the age of twelve He had a thorough knowledge of His divine mission to this earth (cf. v. 49).

Later writers after the New Testament period attempted to fill in from imagination the silence about the childhood of Jesus. The results they achieved are no less than absurd. Luke gives us the only authentic glimpse we have of this period in our Lord's life (vv. 41-52). This picture is evidently a sufficient sample to illuminate for us the so-called "silent years."

Joseph and Mary were accustomed to annually attend the most important of all the Jewish religious festivals—the Passover. It must have been the outstanding event of the entire year in the life of their family. On this particular return trip, Jesus was found to be missing. When finally located He was not "disputing with the doctors," as some have put it, but listening, asking questions and also answering questions Himself. His wisdom was so striking that all who heard Him were "astonished." His first recorded words were, "Wist ye not that I must be about my Father's business?" (v. 49b). Years later, as He died on the cross, He could say of His mission, "It is finished." In the light of this supernatural knowledge concerning His destiny, He yet returned to Nazareth and for eighteen more years was "subject" unto Joseph and Mary (v. 51).

It is of interest to observe that twelve years of age has always been considered by the Jews to be a great turning point in a boy's life.

> At the age of 12 every Jewish boy was styled "a son of the law"; being then put under a course of instruction, and trained to fasting and attendance on public worship, besides being set to learn a trade.[3]

At thirteen the Jewish boy goes out "on his own" and is considered fully accountable to the law, his parents ceasing to be responsible if he breaks it.

---

[3]Robert Jamieson, A. R. Fausett, and David Brown, *A Commentary on the Old and New Testaments,* V, 232.

The chapter closes with the statement that "Jesus increased in wisdom and stature, and in favour with God and man" (v. 52).

The Greek word in this verse translated "increased" would be more literally rendered "kept advancing." The word is used for pioneers hewing down trees and brushwood which obstruct the path of an advancing army.[4]

THE PREPARATION FOR HIS MINISTRY
(3:1—4:13)

The Ministry of John the Baptist (3:1-20)

Verses 1 and 2 contain a most unusual dating of the events now to be related. Tiberius Caesar was the stepson of Augustus. Secular history pictures him as a very evil man. Pontius Pilate was appointed governor (or procurator) of Judaea in A. D. 26 and served in this office for ten years. His position was one of considerable authority as he also commanded the Roman troops stationed there. His office came under the jurisdiction of the governor of Syria.

At the time of Herod the Great's death, his kingdom had been divided among his sons. Archelaus (Matt. 2:22) received approximately half of it. Because of misconduct he was deposed by the emperor after ten years in office and his dominion then came under the Roman procurator. The other half of the kingdom was divided between Herod Antipas and Philip, who thus were "tetrarchs,"

---

[4]*Pulpit Commentary*, XVI, 44.

rulers of a fourth. The former received Galilee as his portion; the latter Ituraea, an area northeast of Palestine, and Trachonitis, which was located between Ituraea and Damascus. A man named Lysanias, of whom little is known, was ruler of Abilene, a small district between Mount Hermon and Damascus.

Annas and his son-in-law Caiaphas are both mentioned by Luke as being the high priests at that time. Annas first served in that capacity but was later removed by the Roman procurator. He was probably looked upon by the people as the true high priest, since the office had originally been for life. Caiaphas, however, was recognized as high priest by the Roman government. The two evidently worked together very closely (see John 18:24; Acts 4:6). Secular history tells us that Annas also had five sons who at different times served as high priest.

During the fifteenth year of the reign of Tiberius, "the word of God" came to John, and he began his ministry as the last and greatest of the Old Testament prophetic line (Matt. 11:13). His service was performed in "all the country about Jordan" (v. 3).

> He seems to have principally preached and taught in the Jordan valley—no doubt for the convenience of his candidates for baptism. But he evidently did not confine his preaching to one spot, or even to one neighborhood. The district here alluded to was about a hundred and fifty miles in length.[5]

5*Ibid.*, 64.

Luke informs us that John, in his ministry, fulfilled the prophecy of Isaiah 40:3-5. Both in the work he did, and in the very place where he worked ("the wilderness") he fulfilled the divine prediction. He called on the people to repent of their sins and seek forgiveness from God, submitting to baptism as a token of their sincerity. In a spiritual sense he thus prepared "the way of the Lord." Though Mark quotes this same prophecy (Mark 1:3) he does not give as much of it. Luke continues the Old Testament statement until he comes to the assertion that "all flesh shall see the salvation of God," a prophecy that will doubtless find its complete fulfillment at the second coming of Christ. Luke's use of the statement is another illustration of the appropriateness of his being called the "Universal Gospel."

It should be carefully observed that John the Baptist called not only for an outward profession of repentance, but for "fruits worthy" of such a claim (v. 8). These "fruits" are defined in a most practical way in verses 10-14. When the people were in danger of mistaking this great prophet for the Messiah Himself, John plainly advised them that they were in error. The Messiah, soon to come, was far mightier than he. When He came, His baptism would not be just a symbolic one with water, but the actual baptism with the Holy Spirit (cf. Acts 1:4-5).

Once again the prophecy passes rapidly from the first to the second advent of our Lord. On Pentecost He baptized with the Holy Spirit. When He comes again He will baptize "with fire" (v. 17; cf. II Thess. 1:8) , and there will be a separation of wheat and chaff.

These teachings were not all that John gave, for "many other things in his exhortation preached he unto the people" (v. 18) . Some of these "other things" are to be found in the gospel of John, chapters 1 and 3. In verses 19-20, Luke gives a parenthetical statement regarding the imprisonment of John by Herod Antipas.

The Baptism of the Son of Man (3:21-22)

With all the other people, John's baptism expressed "repentance for the remission of sins" (v. 3) . The Lord Jesus did not, of course, receive baptism to confess sins, of which He had none (II Cor. 5:21; I Peter 2:22; I John 3:5) . He did by this act, identify Himself sympathetically with sinners who desire a new life. Also, though His baptism did not mark the turning from an old life of sin to a new life with God, it did signalize His consecration to a new phase of His life and service. In addition, by submitting to the baptism of John, He publicly placed His seal of approval on John's ministry in the clearest possible way.

As Jesus prayed, heaven opened and the Holy Spirit "in a bodily shape" (v. 22) descended upon Him. The Bible does not say that the appearance was of a dove, but that the "Holy Ghost descended . . . *like* a dove." The dove represents gentleness and humility. It was also the creature used as a sacrifice by the very poor (see Luke 2:24; Lev.

12:8) . Only on this occasion is the dove used in Scripture as a symbol of the Holy Spirit.

In this marvelous scene, Each of the three Persons of the Trinity is distinctly manifested. The Son is being baptized on the earth; the Spirit descends on Him from above. The voice of the Father speaks from heaven: "Thou art my beloved Son; in thee I am well pleased." Audibly, the heavenly Father shows at the very beginning of the ministry of Jesus Christ that this One who is the "Son of man" is also the divine "Son of God." These words give us complete assurance of the unqualified approval of the Father with regard to the Son's work of redemption.

The Genealogy of the Son of Man (3:23-38)

The genealogy is evidently that of Mary, the mother of Jesus, which proves that Jesus was not only the legal heir of David through Joseph, His foster father, but was also of the Davidic line in a physical way through His mother. All the narrative of the early chapters of Luke is told from Mary's standpoint, just as the nativity record of Matthew is from the viewpoint of Joseph. It is significant that in the Greek, Joseph's name (v. 23) is listed differently from the balance of those in the list. This can be detected in the English version by the use of italics with the remainder of the names. Many commentators feel that the entire statement "being as was supposed the son of Joseph," should be in parenthesis, so that Jesus is actually said to be "the son of Heli." Heli was apparently the father of Mary and the grandfather of Jesus, according to the flesh.

From Abraham to David, this genealogy corresponds to that in Matthew 1. From David to Jesus it is different, this line being traced through Nathan, an obscure son of David, rather than through Solomon. Luke also traces the human ancestry of Jesus all the way back to Adam, in contrast to Matthew who goes only back to Abraham, the progenitor of the Hebrew nation. Matthew obviously was writing especially to reach the Jews; Luke, the Gentiles. When it is said that Adam was "the son of God," it of course does not mean in the same sense that Jesus Christ was. The thought is rather that Adam came directly from the creative hand of God and had no human parent.

This entire passage again emphasizes the fact that Jesus is truly "the Son of man."

The Temptation of the Son of Man (4:1-13)

As the perfect Man, Jesus had to triumph where the first man failed. The contrast between this temptation scene and that of Genesis 3 is striking. Adam had everything in his surroundings, it would seem, conducive to victory. He was dwelling in a lovely garden with every need abundantly supplied. Yet he disobeyed God and yielded to Satan. Jesus was tempted in a "waste howling wilderness." He was surrounded not by tame creatures, but by wild beasts. He was not well fed, but weak and hungry after forty days of fasting. Yet He triumphed utterly over the devil.

Careful readers will observe that in Luke the order of the second and third temptations is reversed from that given in Matthew's gospel. It appears that here Matthew uses the chronological order, the third temptation being peculiarly that to the King and so providing a proper climax in the gospel which emphasizes the kingly aspect of Christ's character. Luke, however, reverses the order of the last two temptations, so that the account closes with the temptation especially aimed at the Lord Jesus as the perfect Man.

The first appeal of Satan was for Jesus to satisfy His hunger by commanding the stones miraculously to become bread (v. 3). This suggestion, on the face of it so simple, was actually exceedingly insidious. Jesus was urged to satisfy a natural and proper desire of the flesh (I Cor. 6:13) by improper means. The Lord Jesus always did the heavenly Father's will (John 8:29). This was *not* His will. Christ worked many wonders while here on earth, but never did He use His deity as a "shortcut," so to speak, to aid His humanity. If He had He would by the very act have stepped out of the place of a true human being, a position which He had voluntarily assumed (Heb. 10:5-10; Phil. 2:6-8). If He had in this instance been willing to relieve His physical suffering by drawing on His divine powers, would He not have done the same at the very cross itself? Thank God for His answer, drawn from Deuteronomy 8:3—"That man doth not live by bread only, but by every word that proceedeth out of the mouth of the LORD." He was indeed hungry but He would wait for His heavenly Father to supply that need in His own good time and way. Observe carefully that Christ was not sharply contrasting spiritual with physical food, as His answer is frequently interpreted. Rather Jesus says, "It is better to be hungry than to be fed without reference to the will of God."[6]

The second appeal of Satan was to show Christ all the kingdoms of the world, and for the usurper to offer Him these kingdoms if He would bow down and worship him. Surely this is the most dastardly word—"worship me"—that the creature could say to the Creator (John 1:1-3). In effect the devil said: "Take all the kingdoms of the world without waiting, without trouble, without suffering." The Lord utterly rejected the temptation by again quoting Scripture. God only is to be worshiped. One day Jesus Christ shall indeed reign as King of kings and Lord of lords. But the suffering had to come before the glory (1 Peter 1:11).

The third appeal of Satan was for Jesus to cast Himself down from the pinnacle of the temple and by miraculous escape from harm demonstrate His divine sonship.

> The height of the eastern wall can be gauged by noting the pinnacle of the temple where the devil took our Lord and told Him to cast Himself down. The drop to the valley of Kidron below is four hundred feet.[7]

Then Satan himself quoted Scripture (Ps. 91:11-12). The Lord Jesus was asked to prove that He was the Son of God by presumptuously entering a place of peril, and then trusting the Father to deliver Him. If in serving God faithfully danger develops, then we are indeed to depend

---

6Morgan, *The Gospel According to Matthew,* p. 32.
7D. A. Thompson, *Jerusalem and the Temples in Bible History and Prophecy,* p. 11.

on Him to deliver us. But never are we to bring ourselves
rashly into a position of danger simply to "show off," to
demonstrate what great faith we have. Again the appeal to
Jesus was to step outside the will of God. Again the
temptation was utterly rejected by the Lord, as He quoted
Deuteronomy 6:16 in answer.

Note carefully that the tempting of Jesus was not in the
sense that we often use the term today, referring not only
to some outward invitation to sin but also to an inward
response from a fallen nature (see James 1:13). This
temptation was in the sense of testing. A new railroad
bridge, rumored to be structurally unsound, was shown to
be reliable when the management lined up locomotives on
it from one side to the other. That was not done to see if
the bridge was strong, but to demonstrate to all that it was
absolutely safe. The Spirit led the Lord Jesus into the
wilderness to seek out this encounter with Satan (v. 1).
The purpose was not to see if the Saviour had flaws, but
rather to demonstrate once for all His perfections.

2

The Words and Works of the Son of Man

(4:14–19:27)

HIS MINISTRY IN GALILEE (4:14–9:50)

He Is Rejected at Nazareth (4:14-30)

VERSES 14 and 15 summarize briefly the opening ministry of Christ. The gospel of John supplies more detail concerning this early ministry. Chapters 2-4 of that book relate the working of His first miracle at Cana in Galilee, the cleansing of the temple and further miracles at Jerusalem, His interview with Nicodemus and His ministry in Samaria. All these events took place before His return to Nazareth which Luke now describes.

The scene takes place in the Nazareth synagogue where the Lord Jesus delivers a most significant message (vv. 16-21). At the synagogues the Jews were accustomed to gather each Sabbath for religious services. They also met there at certain other times during the week, and on special occasions. Children were first admitted to the services at the age of five. After thirteen years of age, they were expected to attend as a legal requirement. The priests and Levites who officiated at the *temple* did *not* do so at the synagogue. There the services were conducted by the ruler (or, elder). If a stranger was present who was known to be a teacher of the Word, it was customary to ask him to read and expound some passage of Scripture. The Bible reading consisted first of a portion from the law, then another from the prophets.

The Lord Jesus on this occasion opened the prophecy of Isaiah deliberately to the portion that we designate now as chapter 61. There He read the great Messianic prophecy found in the first verse and a half. It is striking to observe that He stopped in the very middle of a sentence and, to make it more definite than ever, closed the book. The reason for this is found in the fact that the balance of verses 2 and 3 refers to His second coming, which is yet future. If He had read these words too, He could not have said, as He did: "This day is this scripture fulfilled in your ears" (v. 21).

The people's reaction and the Lord's answer are described in verses 22-27. Although His gracious words amazed them, yet because of their familiarity with Him and His earthly family, they were utterly contemptuous. Jesus used their skepticism as typical of the unbelief of the nation as a whole. He showed that even before this, God had found it necessary to go beyond the boundaries of His chosen nation to find real faith among the Gentiles.

Illustrations were the widow of Sarepta and Naaman the Syrian (I Kings 17; II Kings 5). He clearly implied that such would once again be true and that history would in this respect "repeat itself."

Their contempt changed to fierce anger; the people of Nazareth attempted to throw the Lord Jesus off a cliff. It is said that presently there is a cliff about forty feet high close to the city, and it may be the very place where they tried to destroy Him. However, the Lord, as on other occasions, "passing through the midst of them went his way." Whether His escape was natural or miraculous, we are not told.

It has already been stated that Luke in his gospel dwells especially on the perfect humanity of Jesus Christ, the Son of man. Christ's Nazareth neighbors, however, made the tragic mistake of overemphasizing His humanity. They viewed Him as no more than an ordinary human and, when His claims were greater, they were offended. Some modern teachers make the same mistake of overemphasizing the humanity of Christ.

He Teaches and Heals at Capernaum (4:31-44)

From the hills of Nazareth, Jesus came down to the shores of Galilee and began a ministry at Capernaum (vv. 31-32), the city which had become home for Himself, His mother and His brethren (see Matt. 4:13; 9:1; 11:23; John 2:12).

On the first of these Sabbath days, Christ gave a powerful message at the synagogue. Luke does not give us the actual sermon, nor any part of it, but he tells of the result: "They were astonished at his doctrine: for his word was with power" (v. 32). A demon-possessed man was present. Although there is no record of the Lord speaking first to him, the demon cried out in fear (vv. 33-34). The incident underlines again the reality of demons. It also shows their knowledge of Christ (cf. James 2:19) and their dread that at His first coming He would bring them to their final doom.

Jesus rebuked the demon and required him to hold his peace (v. 35). The time was not yet ripe for His full revelation as the divine Son of God. That realization needed to grow on them gradually until finally at Caesarea Philippi, Peter and the other disciples would make their full confession (Luke 9:18-21). When commanded to come out, the evil spirit obeyed but threw the man "in the midst" (v. 35) as if to cause as much injury as possible before leaving.

After this exhibition the people were amazed even more than before. Because of His authority over demons, they felt that this was indeed a new word from God. Immediately the story of His power began to be talked about by everyone until "the fame of him went out into every place" (v. 37) throughout all of Galilee.

At the conclusion of the synagogue service, Jesus went to the house of Simon Peter. Simon had earlier been introduced to Christ by his brother Andrew (John 1:40-42). On this occasion, Peter's mother-in-law was seriously ill "with a great fever" (v. 38). Jesus, in a moment, so completely healed her that she immediately "ministered unto them" (v. 39). It is obvious from this record that Peter was a married man at the time he met the Lord. Later New Testament revelation indicates that Peter was still married during apostolic days, and that his wife frequently accompanied him on his preaching tours (I Cor. 9:5). According to two of the early church Fathers, Mrs. Simon Peter finally suffered martyrdom, being parted from her husband and carried to her execution. Tradition has it that Peter's last words to her were "Remember thou the Lord."[1]

As the day was closing many sick people were brought to Him, and He healed them all. The diseased were distinguished from the demon-possessed. In New Testament days demon possession sometimes manifested itself in physical phenomena, but it is still quite clear that the majority of those who were ill then, as today, were so from what may be called "natural causes" rather than from supernatural influences.

Early the next morning (which would be the first day of the week), the Saviour arose and went to a solitary place to pray (cf. Mark 1:35). When He was sought out by the people He informed them that He could not tarry but had to go on to the other towns to "preach the kingdom of God" (v. 43). About this preaching He specifically says, "for therefore I am sent." In this manner He fulfilled His Messianic office of prophet, which surely demonstrates the great importance of preaching. While there are doubtless

---

[1]Clement of Alexandria as cited by F. B. Mayer, *Peter: Fisherman, Disciple, Apostle,* p. 185.

other things of importance in our Christian services today, the preaching of the Word of God should always take the foremost place (I Cor. 1:21; II Tim. 4:1-2).

He Calls the First Disciples (5:1-11)

John, in the first chapter of his gospel, records the fact that Peter, Andrew and he himself had already met the Lord and had believed on Him a little before the time of the scene now pictured in Luke 5 (cf. John 1:35-42). Doubtless, the same thing was true of James. At "the Lake of Gennesaret" (another name for the Sea of Galilee) Christ used Peter's boat as a pulpit from which to preach to the crowd on the shore. After the message was over, Peter was commanded to "launch out into the deep" water (v. 4). There he caught "a great multitude of fishes" even though these experienced fishermen had worked all night with no result. This miracle deeply impressed Peter, who then began to see Jesus not only as a great Teacher, even as the Messiah, but as the Son of God, and he realized keenly his own sinfulness.

> The words of Peter exactly express the first feeling of man when he is brought into anything like close contact with God. The sight of divine greatness and holiness makes him feel strongly his own littleness and sinfulness. Like Adam after the fall, his first thought is to hide himself. Like Israel under Sinai, the language of his heart is, "Let not God speak with us, lest we die" (Exod. 20:19).[2]

---

[2]J. C. Ryle, *Expository Thoughts on the Gospels, Luke*, p. 133.

Calming Peter with His loving "fear not," Jesus prophesied that in the future he would "catch men." The literal rendering of the Greek is "take men alive" (v. 10, ASV marg.). This statement is not to be applied directly to every Christian in the sense that all are called to spend full time in evangelistic service. However, it can be claimed as a gracious promise that each believer who faithfully witnesses for his Lord will have the joy of winning souls to Him.

It is striking to note that the first four disciples called by Christ were men from a humble station in life—fishermen, which illustrates the principle enunciated in I Corinthians 1:26-29. The miracle itself has customarily been called "The Miraculous Draught of Fishes." It has long been considered to teach the lesson that fruitfulness comes only from complete dependence on the Lord's word (see v. 5, "at thy word").

He Heals a Leper and a Palsied Man (5:12-26)

By comparison with the gospel of Matthew, the miraculous cleansing of the leper actually took place as Jesus came down from the mountain after His great Sermon on the Mount. The leper had faith in the Lord's power to heal him, but doubted His willingness. As the Lord touched this unclean, ostracized man, immediately the leprosy left him. The man was charged to say nothing of the miracle, doubtless to prevent the gathering of great throngs of mere curiosity seekers who would impede His spiritual ministry. The man was also told to report to the priests for the purpose of putting into effect the laws regarding cleansed lepers (see Lev. 14) .

Some days afterward, Jesus again came to Capernaum where He had previously preached in the synagogue and performed miracles. Quickly the word circulated that He was in the town, and the people began to crowd around the house where He was staying. So many gathered that the house soon was filled even beyond the doors. The Saviour used this opportunity to teach them God's Word, which shows that the main task of His ministry was not to heal the sick but to proclaim the Word.

Then friends brought a palsied man to Jesus. Finding it impossible to get through the crowd to the Saviour, they followed the outside staircase to the flat rooftop, removed some of the tiles, and lowered the man (evidently with ropes) right into the presence of Christ. The surprise of the crowd below, though not mentioned, can be imagined!

Rather than showing any displeasure at such an unorthodox method of reaching Him, Jesus instead observed with favor "their faith" (v. 20) —the faith of the man and his friends. First of all He dealt with the man's sins even before his sickness. If men but realized it, their spiritual condition is of far greater importance than the physical. The palsied man had real faith in the Lord Jesus and, like his ancestor, Abraham, was justified by faith. Christ on this occasion did something more than we as His witnesses are empowered to do. We can tell men that *if* they receive Christ, their sins will be forgiven; but we cannot read their hearts as He could, so as to be absolutely sure that real faith exists there. Knowing for certain what was in each heart, He could authoritatively say, "Thy sins are forgiven thee" (v. 20).

The scribes and Pharisees who were present inwardly began to question the Saviour's right to make such a pronouncement. Of their two questions (v. 21), one is correct, the other false. It is true that no one but God can forgive sins. It is false that Jesus "speaketh blasphemies." He has the right because He is God (Mark 1:1).

Once more the Lord showed His supernatural knowledge. Though these criticisms had not been voiced aloud, yet He "perceived their thoughts" and asked, "What reason ye in your hearts?" (v. 22). He asked them which was easier to *say:* "Thy sins be forgiven thee," or "Rise up and walk." His question did not refer to which was easier to *do* but to *say.* "Thy sins be forgiven thee" is easier to *say* because no one can immediately tell whether it has come true or not. But so they would know He had the power to *do* it as well as *say* it, He then visibly demonstrated that power by healing the palsied man. Their own eyes could observe the evidence so they could then also be sure that what they could not see—forgiveness of sins—had just as truly taken place. The result was amazement on the part of the people. They were compelled to believe that they had seen a wonderful manifestation of God's power, and they glorified Him.

He Calls Matthew and Answers the Criticism of the Scribes and Pharisees (5:27-39)

Again departing from Capernaum, the Lord Jesus passed by the place where Levi (called Matthew in the gospel he wrote) was sitting collecting taxes, probably toll on shipping. When Jesus said, "Follow me," he immediately obeyed. No doubt like the first four called, he had previously heard Christ preach and had believed on Him. Now he was called to full-time service and became one of the twelve apostles. Later he was to write the first gospel record in the New Testament. So one treated by the general public as a despised outcast became the writer of the great gospel directed especially to the Jews.

Shortly afterward Matthew prepared a great feast in his house for Jesus, very clearly for the purpose of introducing his friends to the Lord. The term "sinners" which the Pharisees used (v. 30) was not intended by them in the sense that all have sinned, but rather of social outcasts who openly live in gross sin. The term is sometimes used in the New Testament for prostitutes.

Though not invited to the feast, the scribes and Pharisees intruded and complained, implying that the Lord and His disciples were defiling themselves by eating with such people. The answer of Jesus (vv. 31-32) revealed a clear recognition of the sinful condition of the people. He compared them with those "that are sick." He also revealed His own true purpose—not to endorse their sin nor to participate in it, but rather to act as a spiritual Physician to bring them to God.

When Jesus said, "I came not to call the righteous," He used the word as the Pharisees viewed it. They had a high opinion of their own righteousness. In reality *all* are sinners, but unfortunately some, as the Pharisees, do not realize their need. Christ is doing for these sinners the very thing He came to earth to accomplish—to call them to repentance.

At the same time another question was addressed to the Lord Jesus as to why His disciples did not fast as did the Pharisees and the followers of John the Baptist. His answer was that He, the Bridegroom, was then with them and it was a time for rejoicing rather than for sorrowing, as in fasting. But He prophesied that sadder days would come for His disciples in the future when He would "be taken away from them" (v. 35). This was the first reference to His departure. He continued, "Then shall they fast in those days." Fasting, so prominent in the Old Testament period, was hardly alluded to in the New Testament teaching for this present age. It is not forbidden, but neither is it commanded.

The chapter concludes with two parabolic sayings of Christ, both of which pointed up serious error in the view of the Pharisees. They seemed to think that He had come merely as another great teacher of Israel. As such they felt He would possibly explain more fully but nevertheless would carry on with the old system, the old regime. The Lord showed that instead He had come to bring something absolutely new. He had not come simply to patch up the old garment of Judaism, nor to refill the old "wine bottles," but to inaugurate something entirely new—"new wine must be put into new bottles" (v. 38).

He Answers Criticism That He and His Disciples Are Sabbath-breakers (6:1-11)

On a Sabbath day, possibly the day after the feast at Matthew's house, another controversy arose with the Pharisees. Jesus and His disciples were passing through the wheat fields. As they went the disciples, who were hungry, plucked some of the wheat, separated it from the chaff, and ate it. The Pharisees who were present did not raise any objection to the wheat being taken from the field of another, for that was permitted by the law in such cases (Deut. 23:25). However, they condemned the disciples for doing it on the Sabbath day, which they conceived to be a breaking of the fourth commandment. (That the disciples had not actually broken the commandment is made clear by Christ's statement in Matt. 12:7.)

The answer of the Lord Jesus was intended to reveal to these critics that they had misunderstood the purpose of the whole law, particularly of the fourth commandment. The law was given not to hurt man but to help him. Christ cites the case of David who, while fleeing from Saul, was permitted by the priests to eat of the shewbread in the tabernacle. Ordinarily it was to be consumed by the priests alone. However, this rule was not intended to be so rigidly enforced as to allow people to starve rather than break it. As there was no other food available and David and his men were hungry, this bread was given them without any condemnation on the part of God.

Those little words "have ye not read" (v. 3), were stinging. In effect Jesus was saying, "You who claim to know so much about the Scriptures, have you never noticed at all the deeper implications of the Word of God?" Then He proclaimed Himself "Lord . . . of the sabbath." Once again Jesus claimed for Himself far more than any ordinary mortal could—truly an assertion not only of humanity but also of deity. Some expositors take this statement of the Lord to mean that He had the right if He wished to *break* the law since He was the Lord of the Sabbath. But such an interpretation could not be true since it directly contradicts Matthew 5:17. Christ meant that He was the *authoritative Interpreter* of the law. He knew far more about the real intent and meaning of the fourth commandment than those self-appointed leaders because He was the One who made the Sabbath in the beginning. Thus He was the Lord of the Sabbath.

On another occasion Jesus entered the Capernaum synagogue (v. 6). Once more the critics were watching Him narrowly to see what He would do. They knew that a man with a withered hand was present; they also knew of Christ's ability to heal and of His goodness to those in need. So they evidently expected Him to heal the man even though it was the Sabbath. Their hard hearts knew no concern for the afflicted man in his need; their only thought was to find something in the conduct of Jesus which they could use in an accusation against Him. Whether they had in mind a formal charge against Him before the Sanhedrin, or an accusation to the general public in the hope of damaging His reputation, it is not known.

That which the Lord Jesus did, He did openly before them all. He never did His work "in a corner" (Acts 26:26). He commanded the man with the withered hand to "stand forth" before all the people. Before healing him, however, the Saviour turned to the critics and asked them a soul-searching question, "Is it lawful on the sabbath days to do good, or to do evil? To save life, or to destroy it?" (v. 9). The extremes presented by Christ are jolting. It might be asked, "Is there not a middle course? Is it not possible to do neither good nor evil? To neither save life nor to kill?" The Lord's clear implication was that there was no middle ground. When a person can do good, when one has the opportunity and ability to help others—on *any* day of the week—if he refrains from doing that good, then he does evil. When the priest and Levite passed by the wounded man on the Jericho road (Luke 10:31-32), by not doing good, they did evil. By not seeking to save his life, they incurred at least part of the responsibility for his death.

To the afflicted man Christ spoke in gentleness and mercy: "Stretch forth thy hand." The man then demonstrated his own faith. He had *two* hands, only one of which did he have the power to stretch forth. But he knew what the Lord meant, so he stretched forth the withered hand. As he did, it "was restored whole as the other" (v. 10). Though unable to fabricate any charge against Jesus, the Pharisees, in mad hatred, began to plot His destruction.

He Chooses Twelve Disciples and Gives Them Teaching as to Their Condition in the World (6:12-49)

Before appointing the twelve, Jesus "went out into a mountain to pray." No one knows which mountain this was. When daylight came, He "called unto him his disciples: and of them he chose twelve." Thus there was a direct choice on His part. From among the many disciples who followed Him, He selected these twelve who were eventually to go forth as apostles—"sent ones." Of the twelve, we are already familiar with five, whose call has previously been related by Luke: Peter, James, John, Andrew and Matthew. Philip's introduction to Christ is related in John 1. It is thought by some that Bartholomew is the same person called Nathanael in John 1:45. This may possibly be true, as Bartholomew is not a proper name but actually means "son of Tolmay." Thomas is best known to us as the "doubter" of Christ's resurrection. Little more than the names of James the son of Alphaeus, Judas the brother of James, and Simon "called Zelotes," are known. Judas Iscariot is, of course, well known as the betrayer of the Lord. Iscariot means "man of Kerioth," a place in Judah. So far as is known, he was the only apostle from Judah. All the rest seem to have been from Galilee.

After the apostles were chosen, the Lord came down from the mountain and "stood in the plain." A multitude gathered around Him and many sick and demon-possessed were healed. Then the Lord Jesus gave a striking message, recorded by Luke in verses 20-49. The question often arises: Is this a portion of the famous Sermon on the Mount of Matthew 5-7? The only tenable answer to the question seems to be no. This message was given not on a mountain but "in the plain" (v. 17). Various phrases used here are quite different from those in the Sermon on the Mount, and the law, so prominent in that message, is not referred to at all in this address. Admittedly there are similarities between the two messages, but the Lord Jesus, like other great teachers, gave somewhat similar teachings on various occasions.

This message in Luke's gospel, given just after the selection of the twelve, is a sermon on discipleship. It falls into four divisions:

1. Blessings and woes of discipleship (vv. 20-26). Jesus was not commending such things as poverty and hunger in themselves, but rather when endured "for the Son of man's sake" (v. 22). Neither did Christ condemn riches as such, except when preferred above Him and His will, as in the case of the rich young ruler.

2. The love life of the disciple (vv. 27-38). The disciple is to love all men—enemies as well as friends—and to manifest this love by patience and long-suffering. The disciple's general principle of action is stated (v. 31) and the necessity of his having a higher standard than that of worldly people is made clear.

3. Censoriousness is condemned but conduct is shown to reveal character (vv. 39-45). Verses 39 and 40 contain a warning against false teachers.

4. The peril of knowledge without obedience (vv. 46-49). A profitable comparison can be made between this section and the teaching of James 1:22-25.

He Heals the Servant of a Centurion (7:1-10)

A centurion appealed to Christ, not for himself but for another—a beloved servant who was "dear unto him." The one making the appeal was of course not an Israelite, but a Roman—a Gentile. The Lord Jesus used the incident as typical of His rejection by many in Israel while on the other hand Gentiles received Him by faith (v. 9). This centurion obviously had great confidence in the Lord. He was also a good man—kind to his servant and kind to the Jewish people. Matthew's account of this same miracle (Matt. 8:5-13) represents the soldier as himself coming to Christ; Luke speaks of him sending friends. Either Matthew views what was done by proxy as if it were performed personally, or else, more probably, the centurion did both—first sent friends, then in his anxiety came to Jesus himself.

He Raises the Son of the Widow of Nain (7:11-17)

On the day following the healing of the centurion's servant, the Lord Jesus journeyed to the city of Nain in southern Galilee (this is the sole biblical reference to the town). Luke places considerable emphasis on the great crowd of people who witnessed the wonderful miracle performed in Nain. There were "many of his disciples" present and also "much people" (v. 11). "Much people of the city" were there with the widow in the funeral procession (v. 12). The body of the deceased young man was being carried outside the city for burial, possibly in a nearby cave. The bier (v. 14) was not a coffin such as the Egyptians used, but some kind of couch on which the corpse was laid. The fact that the dead youth was the only son of a widowed mother made the loss especially tragic.

Jesus, moved with compassion for the grieving mother, touched the bier—an act which according to Jewish opinion would make a person unclean. The pallbearers stopped in surprise to see what He intended to do. At Christ's command the young man arose. He began to speak, showing that he was truly alive again.

This was evidently the first time the Lord had restored a dead person to life. As a result, great fear came on all the people. They acknowledged that Jesus was a great Prophet, affirming that "God hath visited his people." But it does not mean that they were necessarily admitting the deity of Christ. The expression is used sometimes in the Old Testament merely to signify that God had in some signal way interposed either to bless or to bring judgment on His people (e.g., Ruth 1:6; I Sam. 2:21; Luke 1:68-69).

He Commends John the Baptist and Condemns the Unbelieving Generation (7:18-35)

Although he had once proclaimed Jesus to be the Messiah, John, now in prison (Luke 3:20), was perplexed. Jesus answered his question by calling to John's attention His wonderworks, which were a fulfillment of Old Testament prophecy (Isa. 35:5-6; 61:1-2).

After disposing of this matter, Christ offered a forceful

vindication of John the Baptist himself. He was no human philosopher (v. 24) or gifted entertainer (v. 25) but a true prophet and, indeed, more than a prophet. Verse 28 explains just why John was "much more than a prophet" (v. 26). However, the statement that "he that is least in the kingdom of God is greater than John" is undoubtedly difficult to interpret. Scofield suggests that such a one is greater "positionally, not morally."[3] Bishop Ryle cogently comments:

> I believe the "least in the kingdom of God," to mean the least believer who lived after the crucifixion and resurrection of Christ. I believe the weakest member of the churches planted by St. Paul, had a clearer knowledge of the exact manner in which God would justify the ungodly than John the Baptist, or anyone who lived before the crucifixion ever could have. The contrast our Lord is drawing, is between the privileges of those who lived to see the great fountain of sin opened by His blood-shedding, and those who died before that blood was shed. We do not realize the enormous difference in the position of these two classes of persons. We do not sufficiently remember how very dimly and indistinctly many great saving truths must needs have been apprehended, before Christ died and the veil was rent in twain. The "way into the holiest was not made manifest," while John the Baptist lived, and for that reason Jesus says that the least member of the Gospel Church was "greater than he." His grace and gifts were not greater, but his knowledge and privileges decidedly were.[4]

[3]C. I. Scofield (ed.), *Scofield Reference Bible*, p. 1010.
[4]Ryle, p. 226.

Following His commendation of John, the Lord gave a condemnation of that generation for refusing to accept either Himself or John. The people were like sulky children who refused to play either "marriage" or "funeral" with their friends (v. 32) —unreasonable, fault-finding, critical. The "wisdom" of verse 35 is very likely a reference to Christ Himself, the divine wisdom (cf. Prov. 8:22-31; I Cor. 1:30). His spiritual children understand both His and John's actions (I Cor. 2:15).

He Is Anointed by the Sinful Woman and Relates the Parable of the Two Debtors (7:36-50)

Whether this scene took place at Capernaum, Nain or some other city, we do not know. We know nothing of the host who entertained the Lord in his home except that his name was Simon, a Pharisee. A brief comparison will make it obvious that this is an entirely different event from that recorded in John 12. The anointing which took place on each occasion was not as unusual as we may imagine. Authorities state that in that day, ointment was frequently used on the feet to keep them from chapping in the hot dry air.

The woman who anoints the Lord is expressly called "a sinner."

The word is the synonym for a harlot. Simon saw a prostitute, to use the blunt word, suddenly cross his threshold. There is no need to emphasize the fact that she had never been there before. No man like Simon, cold and

dispassionate, moral, upright, and conceited, need be
afraid that kind of woman is coming near him! Simon saw
her come in and go round the board, and stooping behind Jesus shed tears over His feet, then with loosened
tresses of her hair wiping them, smothering them with
kisses, and pouring on them precious ointment. Simon
saw this and it perplexed him.[5]

The modern reader may wonder how the woman could
stand behind Jesus and yet anoint His feet (v. 38). The
custom of that day was to recline on couches while
eating.

Verses 39-43 present Simon's perplexity and the Lord's
parable. While Simon had shown a certain degree of
outward respect for Jesus—even inviting Him into his
home for a meal—yet he had not then made up his mind
concerning the Saviour (v. 39). When he saw the sinful
woman anointing the feet of Jesus, he decided that He
could not be a prophet of God or else He would discern
the character of this woman and refuse to have any contact
with her.

As on many other occasions, Christ showed His superhuman power by answering the very thought of Simon's
mind. He related the story of two debtors. The exact
amounts each owed are practically impossible to evaluate
in terms of modern currency. But it is easy to see that one
owed ten times as much as did the other. When the time
for payment came neither could take care of his debt.
Thus far the story was not unusual and could be dupli-
cated in any age and place! But surprisingly the creditor of

5G. Campbell Morgan, *The Parables and Metaphors of Our Lord,* p.
171.

this story freely forgave both debtors and canceled their debts! Which, then, would love him most? Simon was forced to acknowledge that it would be the one forgiven the most.

It is plain that the parable directly applied to Simon and the sinful woman. The Lord in a most amazing way was taking Simon at his own estimate of himself and the sinful woman. He was a Pharisee and, as an orthodox follower of Judaism, would have freely admitted that in the final analysis he, like all men, was a sinner. But he thought of himself as a *little* sinner and the woman as a *big* sinner. Even on such a basis, she, when forgiven, would love the most.

The fact is that Simon did not know the woman as well as he imagined he did. She was a sinner—yes—but she was a *forgiven* sinner! It is evident that she had already been saved by faith, and now was showing her gratitude by coming to the Lord in this way. But, as a matter of fact, there is really no such distinction as little and big sinner in the sight of God. Read and ponder James 2:12; Romans 3:10, 12.

Does the fact that *both* debtors in the parable were forgiven mean that Simon himself was also a forgiven sinner? No. The further words of the Lord show that there was actually no evidence of love on Simon's part. In the parable, one loved *more* than the other, but the second still loved at least to some extent. But then Christ showed that Simon loved not at all, which proves that he really had *no* faith. By omitting the usual marks of courtesy and respect to a guest, Simon had revealed that his heart contained no love for the Master.

> The inference is plain—*only one of the debtors was really forgiven,* though in the first instance, to give room for the play of withheld feeling, the forgiveness of both is supposed in the parable.[6]

Do not fail to notice that although this woman manifested a real love for the Saviour, it was not her *love* which *saved* her, but her *faith* (v. 50).

He Preaches Throughout Galilee and Is Ministered to by Certain Godly Women (8:1-3)

Verse 1 covers in brief words what was evidently an extensive ministry of the Lord Jesus. A note is then added explaining that among the disciples of Christ there were not only men but also certain godly women.

> It was *not* a woman who sold the Lord for thirty pieces of silver. They were *not* women who forsook the Lord in the garden and fled. It was *not* a woman who denied Him three times in the high priest's house. —But there *were* women who wailed and lamented when Jesus was led forth to be crucified. They *were* women who stood to the last by the cross. And they *were* women who were first to visit the grave "where the Lord lay."[7]

Many of the most faithful believers today are women.

[6]Robert Jamieson, A. R. Faussett, and David Brown, *A' Commentary on the Old and New Testaments,* V, 254.

[7]Ryle, p. 245.

Three women are specifically mentioned here. An idea, based on tradition, prevails today that Mary Magdalene was a harlot before she was saved. There is not the slightest hint of that in Scripture. She was indeed oppressed of Satan in a most unusual way, being possessed by seven demons, but other than that we know nothing of her past. The name Magdalene probably is a reference to Magdala, a town of Galilee. Joanna, the wife of Chuza, is mentioned in the Bible only here and in Luke 24:10. There is no other reference to Susanna. Verse 3 reveals that not all the followers of Christ were poor. These three women and "many others" are said to have "ministered unto him of their substance."

He Relates the Parables of the Sower and the Seed, and the Concealed Candle (8:4-18)

In the important parable of the sower and the seed (vv. 4-15), the Sower is Christ Himself in His own earthly ministry and later His witnesses (cf. Matt. 13:37; Acts 1:8). The seed is "the word of God" (v. 11; cf. I Peter 1:23). The soil represents the hearts of those who hear the Word (vv. 12, 15). In each of the four cases mentioned, the seed is the same; the difference in result comes because of the difference in the quality of the soils. The wayside (v. 5) with its trodden-down soil represents hard hearts which refuse to heed the Word. The birds who devoured the seed sown symbolize Satan and his forces who "taketh away the word out of their hearts, lest they should believe and be saved" (v. 12). The rocky ground (v. 6) contained just a shallow bit of soil. The seed sown there seemed to spring up but soon withered away. This speaks of cases where the Word seems to be received "with joy" (v. 13), but is not really taken into the heart—"these have no root." The Word seems in the beginning to produce a result, but this soon fades away. The thorny ground contained good soil in ample amounts but was full of pernicious weeds that soon choked out the good seed (v. 7). These "thorns" are stated to be the "cares and riches and pleasures of this life" (v. 14). Such things are allowed to hold complete sway in the life so that the Word never produces any fruit. The good ground (v. 8) represents honest hearts which hear the Word, keep it, and bring forth fruit (v. 15).

This parable alone makes it clear that there will never be an entirely converted world in this age. Some will not hear the Word. Of those who do, only a minority (one-fourth in the story) will eventually become fruitful for the Lord. Even for these results, however, is it not well worthwhile to preach the Word?

The concealed-candle parable (vv. 16-18) is quite similar to one Jesus told in the Sermon on the Mount (Matt. 5:15-16). The "candle" was actually a lamp (Greek, *luchnos*). "*Luchnos* is not a 'candle' but a hand lamp, fed with oil."[8] It was "a portable lamp usually set on a stand."[9] This lamp plainly speaks of the believer's testimony (Matt. 5:14, 16). It is not to be hidden "under a

---

8R. C. Trench, *Synonyms of the New Testament,* p. 165.
9W. E. Vine, *An Expository Dictionary of New Testament Words,* p. 308.

bed" (v. 16) nor "under a bushel" (Matt. 5:15). One commentator suggests that the bushel represents business; the bed, love of ease. Neither is to be allowed to obscure our testimony for Christ. This is especially true in view of the fact that there is coming a day when all of our works will be tested (v. 17). Christ warns, "Take heed therefore how ye hear" (v. 18). The one who receives God's Word properly and uses what he hears will have still more given him. The one who does not, "from him shall be taken even that which he seemeth to have," as was the case with the seed sown by the wayside (v. 5).

He Reveals the Way of True Spiritual Relationship to Himself (8:19-21)

His mother and brethren apparently came with the purpose of restraining Him. The words of Christ show that *spiritual* relationship is, in the final analysis, more significant than mere *physical* kinship. We must not listen to even our nearest relatives if they seek (even through mistaken love) to draw us away from hearing and doing the Word of God.

He Stills the Stormy Sea (8:22-25)

By this miracle, the Lord Jesus showed His mighty power over inanimate nature. While in a ship with His disciples, a terrific storm arose, and the boat began to fill with water. Though experienced fishermen, the disciples became greatly frightened and awoke the sleeping Saviour.

He arose and rebuked the wind and sea so that a complete calm ensued. The terminology is similar to that used in connection with His casting out demons. Very likely the storm was caused by satanic agency.

Later Jesus rebuked the disciples for having so little faith in Him. The believer who grows exceedingly fearful during the storms of life reveals that his faith is not as strong as it should be. Where they had a few moments before feared the storm, they now feared the Lord. They could not understand, and they said, "What manner of man is this!" On one hand He seemed entirely human, like themselves—He grew weary, He slept. On the other hand, He commanded even winds and water, and exacted instant obedience.

He Casts the Demons out of the Man of Gadara (8:26-39)

Near the city of Gadara, Jesus and the disciples were met by a demon-possessed man. This incident adds a good bit to our knowledge of demonology. Demons are unclean spirits (v. 29). It is possible for more than one demon at a time to indwell a human being (v. 30). A "legion" of demons dwelt within this poor man. "The Roman legion consisted of six thousand soldiers. But the word is used here indefinitely for a large number."[10] Eventually all the demons will be cast into the lake of fire (Matt. 25:41).

At the request of the demons, permission was given them to enter a nearby herd of swine (v. 32). No sooner

---

[10]*Pulpit Commentary,* XVI, 209-10.

had the demons entered than the swine immediately dashed into the sea and were drowned. Apparently a self-respecting hog, unlike some people, would rather be dead than demon-possessed! Our Lord has sometimes been blamed for causing the death of these swine. It should be remembered, however, that He did not command the demons to do this, but simply permitted them to do so. The problem here is no greater than that of why God permits any kind of evil to exist or take place in His universe. It should also be recalled that swine were "bootleg," so to speak, to the Israelites. In a sense Jesus not only freed the man of his demons but also the community of a sinful practice. In the final analysis, surely all will admit that the death of a number of hogs is not to be compared with the restoration of a tormented human to his "right mind" (v. 35).

The swineherds spread the story far and wide, with the result that the people came and asked Jesus to leave their country (v. 37). Like some today, they were more concerned about swine than men.

He Heals the Woman with the Issue of Blood and Raises the Daughter of Jairus (8:40-56)

Jesus then returned to Capernaum and great crowds gathered around Him. Jairus, a ruler of the synagogue there, met Christ with an urgent request. The title "denotes the administrative official, with the duty of preserving order and inviting persons to read or speak in the assembly."[11] Jairus' young daughter was critically ill and about to die. She was twelve years of age—just at the point of coming into maturity.

As Jesus traveled to Jairus' house, a great crowd thronged around Him. In the midst of this mob, a woman with "an issue of blood" pressed close to touch Him. For twelve years this poor woman had suffered from a chronic hemorrhage. In her weakened condition, it must have been exceedingly difficult for her to push through the crowd to Christ.

The coincidence of the two "twelves" is striking. In the home of Jairus, twelve years of sunshine and joy were about to end. The sick woman had completed twelve years of gloom with no hope for any relief from her suffering. Without Christ, the result of each case would have been misery. To both the Lord brought joy for sorrow, beauty for ashes.

After the woman was healed, word came that the little daughter had died, and it was useless to "trouble . . . the Master" further. Jesus spoke words of encouragement to Jairus (v. 50) that have ever since meant much to believers in a similar situation. Then, at the home, Christ took the mother and father into the room and raised the girl back to life again. Verse 54 demonstrates His practical thoughtfulness.

The four miracles recorded in Luke 8 reveal the power of the Son of man over nature, demons, disease and death.

---

[11]Vine, p. 101.

The three recorded instances in which He raised the dead are also very suggestive. All are dead in sin, and only He can give life. Whether it be a child in its comparative innocence; a young man in his youthful vigor, as in the case of the son of the widow of Nain; or one in his maturity, like Lazarus who had been dead for four days, and whose body was in process of corruption—all needed the life that Christ alone could give, and He proved Himself sufficient for each case."[12]

He Sends Forth the Apostles on a Preaching Tour (9:1-10)

The apostles were then given experience under the Lord's personal supervision that would serve them in good stead in the days after His departure. They were empowered by the authority of Christ, and were sent forth to preach and to heal. On the trip they were instructed to refrain from overburdening themselves. They were not to go from house to house like beggars. Their testimony was to be received even as that of the Lord Himself. Luke adds to this section a parenthesis relating the superstitious fear of Herod (vv. 7-9) .

He Miraculously Feeds Five Thousand (9:11-17)

This is the only miracle of Christ recorded by all four of the gospel writers. The people followed after Jesus and broke up the "retreat" to which He had called the apostles after their preaching trip. Having compassion on the

[12]H. A. Ironside, *Expository Notes on the Gospel of Mark*, p. 86.

crowd, He taught them until the day was far spent. Then the disciples suggested that the people be dismissed so that they could go and find food. Jesus ordered them to provide something to eat. They searched and found only five loaves and two fishes—in a boy's lunch. With these the Lord was able to feed the multitude. Without fear of contradiction, it can be said that a mighty miracle took place because all were fed abundantly and yet there was more food left in the end than there had been in the beginning—twelve baskets!

He Receives Peter's Confession, Directly Announces His Death for the First Time, and Teaches the Method of True Discipleship (9:18-26)

On this significant occasion, Jesus first asked what the crowd said about Him. Then He inquired what the disciples themselves had to say on the subject. Peter answered for all that Jesus was "the Christ of God." Jesus then instructed them to "tell no man that thing." The full revelation of His person and work had to wait until after His death, resurrection and ascension. When that time came they were told something quite different (Luke 24:47).

The Lord Jesus, just after Peter's "great confession," told His disciples plainly of His approaching suffering, death and resurrection. His use of the word "must" should be carefully observed. Why did He say that He *must* suffer and die? Because some outside force could be brought to bear upon Him which He was powerless to resist? Absolutely not. On various occasions He proved that no man could lay a hand on Him against His will. It was then a divine compulsion which had Him in its grip. He had to suffer, die and rise because this was the only way lost souls could be saved.

Man, originally created in a perfect condition, had fallen away from God into sin. As a guilty sinner, man had upon him the wrath of a holy God. In His righteousness God had to condemn sinful man, but in His love He provided a way of salvation—*the* one way of salvation— through a Substitute. The Son of God came to this earth and lived a perfect life before men. He did not deserve to die—there was no seed of death in Him, for "the wages of *sin* is death." But He deliberately took upon Himself the sins of men. He "who knew no sin" became "sin for us . . . that we might become the righteousness of God in him" (II Cor. 5:21) .

> There was no other good enough,
> To pay the price of sin,
> He only could unlock the gate
> Of heaven, and let us in.

Christ plainly intimated that He would die on a cross (v. 23) . Anyone who will be His true disciple will also have a "cross" to bear. Being a disciple of the Master involves both negative and positive requirements. On the negative side such a one must deny self. This means more than just giving up a few pleasant things. It means saying no to the self life, to the old nature. On the positive side it means the disciple must "take up his cross." We are not able to emulate Christ's atoning work on the cross, nor do we need to. That work was accomplished once for all and is sufficient for all. "But this man [i. e., Christ], after he had offered one sacrifice for sins for ever, sat down on the right hand of God. For by one offering he hath perfected for ever them that are sanctified" (Heb. 10:12, 14). Those who believe on Him have their sins forgiven. God says, "And their sins and iniquities will I remember no more" (Heb. 10:17). The writer of Hebrews comments: "Now where remission of these is, there is no more offering for sin" (Heb. 10:18). There is no other sacrifice which can be made; no other is needed. Apart from the atonement, however, the cross speaks of complete submission to the will of God, even though it may mean suffering. In this the disciple must imitate his Master. He must "follow Christ" in saying to the heavenly Father, "Not my will, but thine, be done" (Luke 22:42).

The person who tries in a selfish way to "save his life" will end up by finally losing it. The one who gives his life for Christ will prove to be the one who truly saves it. "Only one life 'twill soon be past, only what's done for Christ will last." The question of verse 25 is unanswerable. The conquest of the whole world would be of no profit if the conqueror then entered eternity as a lost soul. Many people of the day were actually convinced that Jesus was the true Messiah, but through fear of men they refused to receive Him. His warning of verse 26 is aimed at such.

He Is Transfigured on a Mountain (9:27-36)

The transfiguration scene provides a foretaste of the coming kingdom (v. 27). Christ appears not in humility but in a glorified state. With Him appears Elijah who well represents saints who pass into glory by rapture rather than by death (I Cor. 15:51; I Thess. 4:17). Moses is also present, representing the "dead in Christ" (I Thess. 4:16) who are raised to share His glory. Peter, James and John may perhaps speak of unglorified men who will still be present on the earth when Christ comes again to establish His kingdom. Even in the midst of this glorious scene there is a prediction of suffering soon to take place (v. 31).

He Relieves a Demon-possessed Child and Again Predicts His Death (9:37-45)

On descending from the transfiguration mount, Jesus relieved a grievous case of demon possession. The contrast is striking—powerful Lord but powerless disciples (v. 40). Matthew adds to Luke's account that the disciples later questioned Christ as to the cause of their failure. They were told it was "because of your unbelief" (Matt. 17:20). The cure He suggested was more prayer (communion with God) and fasting (denial of self).

He Rebukes Pride and Bigotry (9:46-50)

Using the little child as an illustration, Jesus showed the way of true greatness (vv. 46-48). The child is of course to be our example in certain traits only: simple faith, sin-

cerity, dependence on parents. In reproving the action of
John (vv. 49-50) the Lord rebuked a narrow sectarian
spirit. This does not at all mean that we should be
unconcerned about false teachers and unsound doctrine.
We are often warned in the Word of God not to fellowship
with such (note for example John's later warning to a
Christian in II John 9-11).

HIS MINISTRY DURING THE LAST
JOURNEY TO JERUSALEM (9:51—19:27)

He Begins the Journey to Jerusalem and Is Forced to
Rebuke the Disciples on the Way (9:51-62)

In God's great plan the time now approaches when Jesus
Christ was to return once more to heaven's glory. He was
soon to be "received up" (v. 51). But before the ascension,
the predicted suffering and death at Jerusalem had to
come. So with great determination He began the journey
to the holy city to accomplish the passion which He had
already more than once announced. Again on the journey
between Galilee and Jerusalem He passed through the
region of Samaria. Messengers preceded Him to a certain
Samaritan village to prepare for His coming, probably by
making arrangements for Him and His disciples to lodge
there.

When traveling to Galilee on an earlier occasion (John
4), He had been received by some of the Samaritans in a
most favorable manner. Now, however, when He headed
toward Jerusalem, with the Passover drawing near, this

particular village refused to receive Him—doubtless due to the animosity between Samaritans and Jews, with its accompanying rivalry between the Samaritan temple at Mount Gerizim and that of the Jews at Jerusalem.

Because of the discourtesy shown Him, James and John surprisingly suggested that fire be called down from heaven to destroy this town, "even as Elijah did" (probably a reference to II Kings 1). These brothers had a deep love and a strong zeal for the Lord. Unfortunately, however, theirs was "zeal without knowledge"—misguided zeal. Sometimes one meets their counterparts today: people who evidently have a real love for Christ, but seem to manifest too much of a belligerent spirit. To understand what Christ meant when He said, "Ye know not what manner of spirit ye are of" (v. 55), one has but to read Galatians 5:22. Here is the fruit His Spirit seeks to produce in our lives.

The great purpose of the Lord Jesus in this age is expressed in the words "For the Son of man is not come to destroy men's lives, but to save them" (v. 56). How thrilling it is to read later of a time when the Apostle John came to Samaria in an entirely different spirit (Acts 8:25).

In verses 57-62 three typical cases are cited to demonstrate the sad superficiality of some who followed the Lord and aspired to be His disciples. From the answer which Jesus gave to the man speaking in verse 57, it is evident that he had the false conception that following Christ would bring him a great temporal reward. Another person who received a call from the Lord immediately attempted to excuse himself (v. 59). Very likely his father was still living and the true meaning of his words was that he had to wait until after his father died. A third man desired to go home first and follow later. Once again the reply of Christ makes it evident that this man's ardor was rapidly cooling, and he was searching for an excuse to turn back. Whatever his exact situation, it is evident that, like Lot's wife, he did not really want to leave home and follow the Lord.

He Sends out Seventy Disciples as Forerunners on a Preaching Trip (10:1-24)

Since these seventy disciples are not mentioned elsewhere, we are in the dark as to their names. Jesus sent forth this large group to prepare the way for His own coming to "every city and place, whither he himself would come" (v. 1). In view of the great harvest and few laborers, He called on them first to pray, and then to go. While the instructions given were for them on that particular trip, they should be of spiritual help to us also. The seventy were warned of their great peril (v. 3b). They would be persecuted by evil men. On the way they were to avoid luxuries or anything that would impede. Their material support was to be received from children of God to whom they ministered; they were not to go from house to house like beggars. If any city refused to receive them, they were not to attempt to call down fire from heaven. Nevertheless, they were informed that a terrible condemnation does await all such Christ-rejecting sinners.

Indeed, Jesus pronounced an awful judgment on certain cities of His own day which had refused to heed His testimony (vv. 13-16). There is a more severe judgment awaiting Chorazin, Bethsaida and Capernaum than Tyre, Sidon and Sodom, because they had been granted greater light.

A short time later the seventy returned, their mission successfully accomplished (v. 17). The statement of Christ is calculated to warn such lest they become spiritually proud. Although He gave His messengers great power over Satan, they were not to rejoice boastfully over the possession of this power, but rather rejoice over salvation.

Jesus thanked the Father that, although these precious truths of salvation were hidden from the worldly wise, they were revealed to "babes."

He Gives, in Response to a Lawyer's Questions, the Parable of the Good Samaritan (10:25-37)

Since in the theocracy, civil and religious law were one and the same, this lawyer was also an Old Testament scholar. He actually condemned himself with his own words (v. 28). Then he desperately tried to find some loophole of escape by arguing the question of just who his "neighbor" was. In the light of this conversation, Jesus told the story of a poor Jew who, in the hour of his need, was refused help by those who were not only his neighbors but his religious leaders. Later a despised Samaritan befriended the Jew and saved his life.

Actually the Lord Jesus in His teaching went beyond the lawyer's question, showing him that the real issue was not simply "Who is my neighbor?" but "Whom can I be a neighbor to?" Many Jews of that day were said to have despised all who were not members of their own nation. Christ said that any person we can help is our "neighbor." So the command to "love thy neighbor" is really a command to love *all*. Some expositors think that Jesus was actually intending to picture Himself in the character of the good Samaritan. While the narrative certainly makes an effective illustration of that which He does for us, it is doubtful that it was actually intended to be an allegory of His own work.

He Visits Martha and Mary and Shows That Communion with Himself Is the One Absolutely Needful Thing (10:38-42)

Life offers many good and pleasant things. In the final analysis, however, there is but one thing which is absolutely essential—to sit at the feet of Jesus and commune with Him. Many of us today are like Martha. We are so busy serving the Lord (or at least doing what we *think* is service) that we neglect the most important matter of all: our quiet times of communion with Him.

He Teaches the Method and Importance of Prayer (11:1-13)

This is a slightly different version of the so-called "Lord's Prayer" found in Matthew 6, and it was given on another occasion. It should be more properly termed "the disciples' prayer," as the Lord Jesus is the one Person who could not Himself pray it since it says, "Forgive us our sins" (v. 4).

In this model prayer, praise of God and petition for the things of His kingdom come first. Then there is prayer for our own personal needs. In commenting on the phrase "as in heaven" (v. 2), Bishop Ryle reminds us that "heaven is the only place now where God's will is done perfectly, constantly, unhesitatingly, cheerfully, immediately, and without asking any questions."[13]

Following the prayer, Jesus gave a parable which illustrates by contrast the certainty that God will answer the prayer of those who are His children. If a friend who would otherwise refuse a neighbor's inopportune request, will nevertheless, because of the latter's *importunity*, accommodate him, how much more will our loving heavenly Father respond to His children, when we seek, when we knock (vv. 9-10).

A second brief parable shows that the Father will not only respond, but will give us *good* gifts. The best gift of all is the one here mentioned, the Holy Spirit. At that time, however, none of the disciples claimed the promise of verse 13. A bit later the Lord Jesus graciously stated that He Himself would pray for this supreme gift (John 14:16). In response to His prayer, the Holy Spirit was

---

[13]Ryle, p. 8.

given on the day of Pentecost. Since then He comes to indwell each individual who believes on God's Son (Acts 10:44-45). It is interesting to observe that the Lord Jesus, in verse 13, assumed as a fact beyond argument the depravity of the human race. He said: "If ye then, *being evil*, know how to give good gifts. . . ."

He Condemns Blasphemy and Unbelief (11:14-36)

Jesus relieved a very serious case of demon possession in such a way as to make the people wonder (v. 14). Some of those present, however, blasphemed by attributing His divine power, which they were unable to deny, to Satan. Others in rank unbelief had the audacity to ask for "a sign from heaven." The complaint of verse 15 was answered by the statement of Christ in verses 17-26; the request of verse 16 in verses 29-36.

He answered the blasphemy of ascribing His work to the devil's power by two arguments: (1) Satan is not divided against himself (vv. 17-18). (2) Others—even their own children approved by them—attempted to cast out demons (v. 19). By whose power were they working? (It should be observed that the Lord neither attacked nor defended these exorcists.) The "strong man" of verse 21 is Satan himself. The "stronger" (v. 22) is Christ. If He is able to overcome Satan, He must be working by the Spirit of God and therefore should be accepted. Actually there is no neutrality in regard to Jesus Christ. The one who refuses to receive Him is really rejecting; the one who refuses to "gather" with Him is actually "scattering" (v. 23).

Jesus graphically pictured a person from whom a demon had gone out. His words provide considerable information on the mysterious subject of demonology. The demon-possessed person of whom Christ spoke typifies the unbelieving generation as a whole. The Lord cast demons out of individuals—this demonstrates His supremacy over Satan and his kingdom. Even now He is controlling Satan's power. But if the generation refuses to take the final step of receiving Him, all is without avail. The last state will be worse than the first (v. 26). The habitation from which the demon had gone was "swept and garnished" but *empty*. There must be some stronger Person in control to keep the demons out, otherwise the end condition will be more hopeless than the beginning. That stronger power is the Lord Jesus Christ Himself. If He is within, then it can truly be said of the redeemed one: "Greater is he that is in you, than he that is in the world" (I John 4:4).

As He was answering these objectors, Jesus was interrupted by an emotional outcry from a woman who was present (v. 27). Evidently pleased with His teaching, she cried out as to the blessedness of the mother of such a Son. The Lord used this incident as the basis for a most striking and important teaching. He observed that the one who knows the Word of God and obeys it is more blessed than the one who simply happened to be born into the physical family of Christ when He was here on earth.

We cannot doubt that the words of this verse were spoken with a prophetic foresight of the unscriptural wor-

ship of the Virgin Mary, which was one day to arise and
prevail so extensively in the Church of Christ. By no
ingenuity, or torturing process, can the words be made to
bear any but one plain meaning. They declare, that to
hear the Word of God and keep it, is to be more blessed
than to be connected with Christ by the ties of flesh, and
that to be the mother of Christ according to the flesh does
not confer on any one greater honor and privileges than
to believe and obey the Gospel.[14]

The request of verse 16 for a sign was answered by a
condemnation of the entire generation (v. 29). The
attitude of the people as a whole was well represented by
this asking for a sign. They had had an abundance of signs
already, but still they sought more. What they really
wanted was not an encouragement to faith but additional
material to criticize. Christ refused at that time to give a
sign but He promised one great evidence in the near
future—His resurrection from the dead. Of that resurrection the story of Jonah is a type. The Ninevites of Jonah's
day, and the Queen of Sheba who once visited Solomon,
will some day condemn that unbelieving generation.
Although Gentiles with comparatively little spiritual light,
these people were touched by God's dealing with them. But
though Jesus Christ is greater than Jonah or Solomon, yet
His own covenant people refused to heed the full light He
had given them. Verse 33 emphasizes the importance of
using the light which one has—a further rebuke to His
generation which had not done this.

[14]*Ibid.,* p. 35.

In verses 34-36 "once again, He took the illustration of the eye. The subject He was illustrating was the necessity for singleness of motive in life, having one aim, purpose, passion."[15] The physical sight is here used as a figure of the spiritual vision. The eye is the lamp which brings light into the body. If the eye is "single"—clear and not out of order—then the whole body is full of light. On the other hand, if the eye is "evil"—the word does not refer to moral wickedness but to being "out of order"—then the very light is warped and twisted so that the body is "full of darkness." These people had been given abundant light, but their spiritual and moral vision was, sad to say, warped and twisted. When one has sound spiritual vision, then he will not only be full of light himself, but will be like a lamp to give light to others (v. 36).

He Condemns the Pharisees for Hypocrisy (11:37—12:12)

The unnamed Pharisee of verse 37 was evidently very similar to the one mentioned in 7:36. Although not a true believer in Jesus, he showed a certain degree of outward respect for Him and invited Him into his home for a meal. Perhaps intentionally in order to provoke the discussion that follows, the Lord refrained from washing before the meal.

An elaborate system of utterly meaningless ablutions, each carried out with particular gestures, had been instituted by the rabbinical schools. All these senseless forms and ceremonies had been developed out of the original

[15]Morgan, p. 20.

simple directions to secure cleanliness in the Levitical
Law . . . The Talmud has many references to these
practices.[16]

Jewish tradition tells of one rabbi who died of thirst
rather than forego these formal washings. During the New
Testament period, it is said that some people believed that
a demon sat on hands which were not properly washed.

Jesus used the occasion to administer a severe rebuke to
formalism and hypocrisy in religion. His statement "But
rather give alms of such things as ye have; and, behold, all
things are clean unto you," is difficult of interpretation.
However, it certainly does *not* mean that if a person is
generous in his gifts to the poor this will blot out other sins
he may have committed. The thought probably is that if
we offer as a gift to God that which we actually have to
contribute—our hearts, our bodies as a "living sacrifice"
(Rom. 12:1)—then all of the other things we undertake to
do will necessarily be in proper order.

The Pharisees, like some religious people today, while
closely adhering to the less significant features of religion,
missed the most important things—justice and the love of
God (v. 42). In reality, they were hypocrites loving the
praise of men more than the praise of God.

A lawyer then interrupted Jesus (v. 45). The lawyers of
that day were the professional teachers of the Mosaic law
who attempted to expound difficult points to the people. It
should be remembered that in contrast to our time, their
civil law was the same as their *religious* law, so lawyers

---

[16]*Pulpit Commentary*, pp. 306-7.

were of necessity students of the Bible—the Old Testament. Some of these lawyers were connected with the Pharisees, some with the Sadducees. This particular man was obviously closely associated with the Pharisees. Jesus pronounced woe on the lawyers also. They laid down all kinds of burdensome and vexatious regulations which they taught as essential to salvation, yet they themselves gave little heed to those rules they placed on others. They professed to honor the prophets of old. Yet they showed by their conduct that their real state of mind was the same as that of their ancestors who had murdered those prophets. The final reckoning for the martyrs and prophets Israel had already slain and would yet slay would be required of that generation, prophesied the Lord (vv. 50-51). This prediction was overwhelmingly fulfilled in the tragic destruction of Jerusalem in A. D. 70.

The final condemnation of the lawyers was a terrible one. They had hindered instead of helped people to come to God; they had "taken away the key of knowledge" instead of giving it to men.

Again the Lord Jesus warned against the "leaven of the Pharisees" which He plainly declared to be *hypocrisy* (12:1). Even hidden wickedness would some day be revealed. Because of this, the friends of Christ were not to fear wicked persecutors, but rather to fear God. Our God is concerned with even the smallest details of His creation —the tiny bird, the little hair. Therefore we can be sure that He watches over His people who "are of more value than many sparrows" (v. 7).

The blasphemy against the Holy Spirit (v. 10) was the sin of seeing the Son of God Himself work His mighty miracles in the power of the Holy Ghost and then to reject Him and attribute these works to Satan (see Mark 3:28-30).

He Warns Against Covetousness and Anxiety but Encourages Watchful Expectation of His Return (12:13-59)

Again Christ was interrupted in His teaching, this time by a covetous man. The latter's request was used as the basis for a warning to all. This man wanted the Saviour to settle a dispute between himself and his brother over certain temporal affairs. Jesus absolutely refused to intervene in such a matter. His work was not to settle petty secular grievances; He came to teach great spiritual truths and to provide a marvelous spiritual salvation. How sad that one could hear from the mouth of our Lord these magnificent religious teachings and still be concerned only with worldly things! Christ's answer makes it plain that this man was not truly seeking justice, as he pretended, but was really covetous—avaricious, wanting more than was rightfully his. How needed in our own day is the truth that "a man's life consisteth not in the abundance of the things which he possesseth" (v. 15).

To illustrate this fact Jesus told one of His most striking and best known parables, that of the rich fool (vv. 16-21). Only Luke records this story. The man of whom the Lord told was doubtless considered by the world a very wise man. But in God's sight he was a fool. His concern was only with *things*—"*my* fruits," "*my* barns" "*my* goods"— even "*my* soul." Suddenly and without warning he was called to face the God whom he had never given a place in his life. All of his things had to be left behind. He had lived for self only. Though counted rich by the world, he was an utter pauper when it came to the true riches.

In the light of this parable, Christ's disciples were warned against worldly anxiety and worry (vv. 22-34). They were to depend completely on the heavenly Father, and to lay up treasure in heaven rather than on earth.

Jesus went on to use additional parables to emphasize the importance of watchfulness in view of His return (vv. 35-48). The amazing promise of verse 37*b* is probably not to be taken literally. Peter inquired (v. 41) as to whether this teaching was only for the twelve or for all disciples. The Lord answered him with a question of His own and with another parable. By this He made it clear that the teaching was for *all* in the household of God, which during the present age is the church. Though His teaching here is applicable to all believers, it is especially appropriate to those in positions of leadership and authority. Verse 45 has, sad to say, been literally fulfilled in church history. A real belief in the Lord's return is obviously of great practical importance in the daily life of the Christian.

After speaking of the necessity of being prepared for His second coming, Jesus summed up certain results of His first advent (vv. 49-53). The "fire" of verse 49 symbolizes trouble and affliction (cf. Lam. 1:13; Ezek. 39:6; Hosea 8:14; Amos 2:2, 5). Because of the wickedness of men's hearts, the Saviour's coming to earth had created division between those who received Him and those who would not.

A rebuke was administered "to the people" (vv. 54-59). The Messianic signs were being fulfilled before their very eyes, yet they were unable to discern them. The little parable with which the message closes illustrates the necessity of getting right with God. When one knows he is in the wrong, he had better settle things "out of court." When the day of final judgment arrives, it will be too late.

He Teaches the Necessity of Repentance (13:1-9)

The occasion for this teaching was provided by two startling events of the day. Further details of these happenings are not known beyond the few words recorded here. Once again only Luke records the parable found in verses 6-9. This was a warning first of all to the nation Israel. It should, however, also be applied to individual lives of those who claim to be God's servants. The illustration very clearly condemns unfruitfulness.

He Heals the Woman with a Spirit of Infirmity, and Teaches the Parables of the Mustard Seed and Leaven (13:10-21)

In a synagogue, the Lord saw one who, like Job, was physically afflicted by Satan, even though a woman of faith (v. 16). Graciously and unasked, He healed her, but was severely criticized by those who had scrupulous concern for rules and regulations but no real love or sympathy in their hearts for suffering humanity.

The parable of the mustard seed (vv. 18-19) speaks of the large but, to a considerable extent, unnatural growth which the kingdom will experience during this age. Church history is a sufficient commentary on the parable. The picture in the parable of the leaven (vv. 20-21) is that of the meal offering, in which leaven was absolutely prohibited (see Lev. 2:1, 4, 11). The "three measures" are specifically named in Leviticus 14:10 ("three tenth deals"). Meal represents the perfect doctrine of Christ; leaven speaks of evil doctrine secretly introduced into the true teaching. This situation is often to be found in Christendom today.

He Warns Men to Seek the Lord While He May be Found (13:22-35)

Jesus continued on His journey to Jerusalem, teaching as He went (vv. 22-30). The question "Are there few that be saved?" perhaps reflects the idea that all Israelites would be saved, but no other people. The Lord's warning (vv. 24-25) refers to the time when the age of grace will finally end and it will be too late to seek Him. As in previous teachings, He once more emphasized the insufficiency of knowledge alone, and made it clear that salvation is an *individual* matter. Merely to be a member of the nation descended from Abraham, Isaac and Jacob is not enough to entitle one to a place in the future kingdom.

Verse 33 explains in large measure the rather mysterious statement of verse 32. "To day and to morrow, and the third day" was evidently a way of saying "a short time." In His death and resurrection Jesus was *perfected* in the sense of becoming a perfect Saviour.

In His lament of verses 34-35, the city of Jerusalem was used to personify the whole nation. The time when Israel acknowledges Jesus to be the true Messiah had not yet come but, according to prophecy, is sure and certain.

He Heals a Man with Dropsy, and in the House of a Pharisee Tells the Parable of the Great Supper (14:1-24)

The lawyers and Pharisees criticized the healing of the sick man because it was done on the Sabbath day. How quickly Jesus showed up their inconsistency (v. 5) !

Jesus then condemned self-seeking while exalting humility and unselfishness (vv. 7-14) . Sometimes, at least, it is true that "bad manners are bad morals." Discourtesy of the type Jesus observed in the Pharisee's house (v. 7) reveals a wrong heart condition. He, therefore, uttered first a warning "to those which were bidden." Then, beginning with verse 12, He gave an admonition "to him that bade him," encouraging liberality and unselfishness. His teaching does not mean that we should never invite our friends to our homes for hospitality. The thought is that *all* of our goodness should not be shown just to those from whom we expect something in return. If our hearts are truly right, we will show kindness to all, regardless of whether or not we think they can ever repay us.

The parable of the great supper (vv. 15-24) pictures a host who did the very thing Christ has just commended. The host, of course, represents God Himself. By primary application, the people invited were the Israelites. When they rejected the Lord, He then turned to the Gentiles. But a secondary application can be made to anyone today who rejects the invitation to salvation. The parable itself is introduced by the exclamation of one present: "Blessed is he that shall eat bread in the kingdom of God" (v. 15). Jesus tacitly agreed with this statement, but went on to show that many foolishly refused to have this great blessing even though it could be freely theirs.

He Reveals the Conditions of True Discipleship (14:25-35)

After He left the Pharisee's house "great multitudes" followed Jesus. They were attracted to Him and were interested in His teaching. But—could He count on them as true disciples? (For that matter, can He count on us?) His words in these verses have to do not with salvation but with true discipleship. Thrice over the Lord said that the one who does not follow the conditions here specified "cannot be my disciple" (vv. 26-27, 33). These all-important conditions are:

1. The true disciple must "hate . . . father . . . mother . . . and his own life also" (v. 26). In the Hebrew idiom, to love one thing and "hate" another means to love one much

more than the other (see Matt. 6:24; Rom. 9:13; Gen. 29:30-31). The true disciple must love Christ much more than relatives or even than his own life.

2. The true disciple must "bear his cross" (v. 27). He must say to the Father, "Not my will but Thine." The *cross* speaks of complete submission to the Father's will.

3. The true disciple "forsaketh all that he hath" (v. 33). This does not mean immediately giving up all possessions and leaving all relatives. It does mean "that a man cannot be Christ's disciple unless he is deliberately prepared to give up everything for His sake, if need be, and to encounter any enemy, and make any sacrifice."[17]

The little parables of the unfinished tower (vv. 28-30) and the defeated army (vv. 31-32) should not be interpreted as meaning that one should "count the cost" of discipleship and then decide *not* to follow Christ. They rather speak of the Lord as the One who is constructing a building and fighting a battle. "Therefore" (v. 33, ASV) He must have followers on whom He can depend—He must have true disciples. The closing verses in the passage warn of the danger of a true disciple losing his testimony (cf. Philemon 23 with II Tim. 4:10).

He Teaches Parables Concerning the Lost Sheep, the Lost Coin, and the Lost Son (15:1-32)

Before interpreting these parables it is necessary to notice carefully the background of the teaching. The publicans and sinners flocked to Christ (v. 1); the self-

---
[17]Ryle, p. 172.

righteous Pharisees criticized (v. 2). The Lord Jesus
answered them with three parables, each of which emphasized the joy over one lost but now found (vv. 7, 10, 32).
The "ninety and nine just persons" of parable one and the
"elder son" of parable three represent the self-righteous
who refuse to come to Christ. It has been suggested that the
parables emphasize respectively the work of the Son, the
Holy Spirit, and the Father, though the second parable is
not quite so clear in this respect as the other two.

It may seem incongruous that the woman would have
even called in her neighbors to rejoice over the finding of
the coin. But this is explained by the fact:

> These pieces of silver were joined together in a chain
> and given by the husband to seal the marriage ceremony.
> They were worn across the wife's forehead and valued as a
> wedding ring is among us. If one coin should be lost it
> was thought to indicate the wife's unfaithfulness to the
> husband.[18]

The parable of the lost son, popularly called "the
prodigal son," may also well be used to illustrate the
backsliding Christian who is ready to confess his sins and
to be restored to fellowship with the Father (I John
1:9).

He Illustrates with Parables the Right and Wrong Uses of Money (16:1-31)

Christ continued the message of the previous chapter,
especially addressing the disciples (v. 1). He illustrated

---

[18]Ironside, *Addresses on Luke,* p. 490.

the right use of money by the parable of the unjust steward who, realizing that he would shortly lose his position because of his dishonesty, used the authority he still had to make friends who would later help him in his need. The lord (*"his* lord," v. 5, ASV) —*not* Christ but the steward's master—was forced to commend the man, not for his honesty but for his wisdom. Jesus was not at all praising dishonesty, but rather teaching that we should use our money with wisdom. We should "make . . . friends by means of the mammon of unrighteousness" (v. 9, ASV) , so that we may some day have these friends to receive us "into everlasting habitations." A practical example would be money given to Christian missions to win lost souls to Christ. It is generally agreed that "mammon" refers to wealth or riches, but the origin of the word is obscure. It is said by some authorities to be derived from the name of a pagan god of wealth. G. Campbell Morgan states that when money is termed "the mammon of *unrighteousness"* the word means neither wicked nor good. Money is "nonmoral" in itself and can be used either for good or for evil.[19]

The covetous Pharisees derided this teaching, and were condemned for their evil hearts of unbelief and for their loose ideas regarding marriage (vv. 14-18) . "Presseth" in verse 16 (AV) is rendered "entereth violently" in the American Standard Version. The statement probably refers to those trying to force their way into the kingdom when their hearts are not truly right with God.

---

[19]Morgan, p. 220.

The chapter closes with the narrative of the rich man in hell (vv. 19-31). The story possibly relates a true occurrence but is used in a parabolic way, as an illustration of the wrong use of money. The rich man lived selfishly for wealth and worldly things. In the end, the saved beggar proved to be far richer than the unsaved man of wealth. This narrative proves the reality of hell. The truth of verse 31 has since been demonstrated—One did indeed rise from the dead, but many still refuse to believe. "The spectacular and the miraculous will not have any effect upon the life of men and women if the moral has failed to appeal."[20] If men's hearts refuse to respond to the clear, plain teaching of the Word of God, they will not be touched by the miraculous.

He Teaches Concerning Responsibility, Forgiveness, Faith and Humility (17:1-10)

The Lord Jesus had just spoken to the Pharisees. Then He spoke again to the disciples, this time concerning the importance of one's responsibility to others (vv. 1-2). With human nature and the world what they are, it is to be expected that some will cause others to stumble. This does not, however, excuse the offenders. A spirit of forgiveness is commanded in verses 3-4. If one is injured he should go directly to the person involved and settle it with him. If this one asks forgiveness it should be granted even "seven

---

[20]*Ibid.*, p. 227.

times in a day." This teaching made the disciples realize their need of greater faith (vv. 5-6), so they requested, "Increase our faith." "They never spoke more intelligently than they did in that moment."[21] Christ's answer reveals that it is not the quantity of their faith that needs increasing but the quality. A grain of mustard seed, though small, contains real *life* within. Nothing is impossible to faith which has real life in it, even though that faith be no larger than "a grain of mustard seed." The closing injunction concerns humility (vv. 7-10). This is a warning to us not to become proud if through faith we do accomplish real service for God.

He Cleanses Ten Lepers but Only One Returns to Give Thanks (17:11-19)

He then journeyed "through the midst of Samaria and Galilee" (v. 11). This probably means that He followed the border between the two sections over to Jordan and thence down to Jericho. The lepers were commanded, "Go and show yourselves unto the priests" (v. 14, ASV). In the Mosaic law the priests were appointed to judge whether a person actually had leprosy (Lev. 13-14). These lepers understood Christ's implication that if they obeyed this command the priests would find them to be clean. Of the ten healed, evidently only one was actually saved by faith, and that one a Samaritan.

---

[21]Morgan, *The Gospel According to Luke,* p. 190.

He Teaches Concerning the Kingdom and His Second Coming (17:20-37)

In answer to a question from the Pharisees, Christ stated that God's kingdom was not to be seen by His enemies (vv. 20-21). The Greek word translated "observation" is said to "always mean the watching of hostility."[22] "Within you" by literal translation should read "among you." Though these enemies of Christ did not see it, the kingdom was even "among them." "Meantime, the kingdom was actually 'in the midst' of the Pharisees in the persons of the King and His disciples."[23]

The admonitions and warnings in view of the Lord's return (vv. 22-37) are similar to the teachings in Matthew 24. The reference to "the days of the Son of man" in verse 22 has to do with the time when Jesus Christ was present on the earth in the flesh. The same expression in verse 26 refers to the time when He shall return and once more be on the earth in the flesh. The period just preceding His return will be one of unconcern for God and His claims, even as in the days of Noah before the flood, and of Sodom before its destruction. In its present context, verse 31 was apparently a warning against attachment to the world system in that day, even as Lot's wife was attached to wicked Sodom. Verses 34-36 speak of a taking away of some in judgment when Christ returns. The Battle of Armageddon is probably referred to in verse 37. The body (or

---

[22]*Ibid.*, p. 200.
[23]Scofield, p. 1100.

corpse) signifies corruption of death, the eagles are the vultures (cf. Rev. 19:17-18) .

He Gives Two Parables About Prayer (18:1-14)

The parable of the unjust judge (vv. 1-8) teaches by means of contrast, revealing God's attitude to prayer. If a conscienceless judge will grant justice to a humble supplicant because of her persistence, how much more will a holy God hearken to His people when they call on Him! Since He *will* hear, therefore "men ought *always* to pray." Prayer will be needed down to the very moment of the second advent, for even at that time there will be adverse conditions here on earth (v. 8) .

The parable of the Pharisee and the publican (vv. 9-14) shows what man's attitude toward prayer ought to be. Prayer is of little value if the heart has a wrong attitude. The prayer of a person like the one mentioned in verse 9 is utterly worthless. On the other hand, if a humble repentant sinner comes to a merciful God, he will find that the Lord is "on the giving hand."

He Receives Children, Instructs the Rich Young Ruler, and Heals a Blind Man (18:15-43)

While receiving little children, Christ used them as an example of the attitude necessary if one would enter the kingdom of God (vv. 15-17) —childlike simplicity, humility, faith.

The rich young ruler refused to follow the Lord because

of a love for wealth (vv. 18-30). The Lord Jesus used the occasion to show that real love and service to Himself would certainly be rewarded (vv. 28-30).

He again predicted His death but the disciples did not understand (vv. 31-34).

> After all we have no right to wonder at the disciples being slow to understand the first advent of Christ in humiliation, when we see how many Christians refuse to acknowledge the second advent in glory, although the texts about Messiah's glory are far more numerous than those about His sufferings. Above all, we have no right to wonder when we see how many, even now, are utterly in the dark about the true purpose of Christ's death upon the cross.[24]

The Lord Jesus performed a miracle of healing on a blind man as He came near Jericho (vv. 35-43). This man had real faith in Christ (v. 42) and was not only healed physically but saved spiritually.

He Is Received by Zacchaeus the Publican, and Gives the Parable of the Pounds (19:1-27)

A rich man was then saved, strikingly illustrating the teaching of Christ in 18:27. As the man was already deeply interested, the Lord's gracious dealing with him completely won his heart. The result was that he "received him joyfully," not only into his home but also into his heart.

---

[24]Ryle, p. 283.

His statement in verse 8 is convincing evidence of a true conversion.

The parable of the pounds (vv. 11-27) can best be understood in the light of the background described in verse 11. Jesus showed that He was not going to establish the kingdom immediately. Instead He was going away to receive a kingdom. Later He would return and establish His reign. Meantime He was leaving His servants with the responsibility of "occupying" till He comes. The parable of the talents in Matthew 25 is quite similar. However, in that story different amounts were given, signifying different abilities and opportunities. Here the same amount— one pound—is given to each servant. Each person who serves Christ has, in one sense, the same thing—one life to live for Him. Eventually the servants were rewarded according to the degree in which they had used their one pound for the king.

3

The Suffering and Atoning Death
of the Son of Man

(19:28—23:56)

HE ENTERS JERUSALEM AMID PUBLIC ACCLAIM
AND CLEANSES THE TEMPLE (19:28-48)

THIS JOYOUS SCENE took place on the day we usually call
Palm Sunday. When Jesus visited Jerusalem on other
occasions, He entered the city quietly and without pub-
licity. But here He came to initiate the sequence of events
which would take Him to the cross in a few days. No doubt
He deliberately allowed this public acclamation so as to
call the attention of all to Himself in His death—"Behold
the Lamb of God, which taketh away the sin of the world"
(John 1:29). While all four gospel writers tell of this
incident, Luke adds the touching picture of Christ weeping over Jerusalem (vv. 41-44).

He Answers Various Difficult Questions
from His Enemies (20:1—21:4)

He Answers the Question Concerning His Authority (20:1-8)

The rulers demanded proof of His authority for doing "these things." They referred to the various details in connection with the entrance into the city, but especially to His cleansing of the temple. They realized that this action was a condemnation of their own lack of faithfulness in keeping God's house pure. Jesus countered with a question of His own. Was John's teaching, symbolized by his baptism, directly from God? Or was it purely a human doctrine without divine sanction? In other words, was John a true prophet, or not? The leaders, having rejected John's message, were unwilling to admit he was a real prophet for they would then have condemned themselves. On the other hand, they hesitated to term him an imposter for, even though he was dead, the people as a whole still venerated him as a true man of God. When they, therefore, refused to answer Jesus' question, He refused to explain the basis of His authority.

He Tells the Parable of the Wicked Husbandmen (20:9-19)

This parable clearly speaks of their rejection of Him. Note carefully verse 16: "He shall come and destroy these husbandmen, and shall give the vineyard to others." Up to this time, salvation had centered in Israel, but in the new age this would no longer be true. God would then "visit the Gentiles, to take out of them a people for his name" (Acts 15:14).

He Answers the Question Concerning the Tribute to Caesar (20:20-26)

They then asked Him about the rightness of paying tribute to a Gentile king. No doubt they felt that their cunning question would leave Him in a dilemma. If He approved the paying of taxes to Caesar, it could injure His popularity with the masses. On the other hand, if He condemned the practice, as they apparently thought He might (v. 20), then they could accuse Him of subversive teaching. By the simple expedient of calling attention to a Roman denarius, Jesus indicated that they were getting some benefits from human government and therefore should give government its due (see Rom. 13:7). At the same time the Lord gave them an answer they did not ask for—"Render . . . unto God the things which be God's." Greater even than our responsibility to human government is our responsibility to God. Like many today, these questioners were evading their responsibility to God.

He Answers the Question Concerning the Resurrection (20:27-40)

The Sadducees, the rationalistic religionists of the day, presented a question about the resurrection. If a woman had been married to seven husbands in this present life, whose wife would she be? That the question was not an honest one is made clear by the fact that the Sadducees did not believe in resurrection at all and, therefore, would have had no problem in such a case as that cited. Nevertheless, the Lord gave a clear and enlightening answer. Marriage and sexual relations, such as we know them in this world, will not exist in the resurrection life, any more than they do now among the holy angels. Apparent problems such as that suggested do not really exist. At the same time the Lord Jesus strongly affirmed the reality of the resurrection, which the Sadducees denied.

He Warns His Disciples of the Scribes (20:41-47)

Christ Himself asked a question which the scribes were unwilling to answer. He showed that Psalm 110:1, admittedly Messianic, presents King David calling his own Descendant (the Messiah) "my Lord." Only the deity of the Messiah could account for David calling his "son" his Lord. Thus it is shown that even the Old Testament teaches the deity of Christ, the very claim for which the leaders condemned Jesus.

He Commends a Widow for Her Sacrificial Offering (21:1-4)

This familiar incident reveals that it is not merely the amount of the gift given to God's work that counts, but the proportion given in relation to that kept for self. The sum given by the poor widow was evidently all the money she had for that day, so that she, doubtless, went hungry to make this small contribution. Representing a real sacrifice, it was larger in God's sight than much larger amounts which were not even missed by wealthy donors.

He Gives a Last Prophetic Message
(21:5-38)

Each of the Synoptic Gospels presents a portion of the great prophecy, the Olivet Discourse. Matthew's account (chaps. 24-25) is the most complete. However, the gospel of Luke contains a part of the discourse that neither Matthew nor Mark record. The teaching of the Lord on this occasion was in answer to questions from the disciples concerning the destruction of the temple and His second coming. The account in Matthew has to do exclusively with the return of Christ. Mark contains a similar but briefer account. Only Luke records the portion which tells of the imminent devastation of Jerusalem and the temple.

In the present chapter, verses 8-19 picture the sufferings of Jesus' disciples during the time between His ascension and the overthrow of Jerusalem. While verse 16*b* may at first seem to be contradictory to verse 18, careful thought will show that both can be true. The Lord does not always deliver His people from *temporal* trials; some have even been allowed in God's purpose to suffer death by martyrdom. But in the final sense the one who trusts in Christ will "never perish" (John 3:16) and this applies even to the very hairs of his head.

The destruction of Jerusalem and the temple, graphically related in verses 20-24, became an actuality in A. D. 70, less than forty years later, when Titus the Roman general (later emperor) demolished the city. Over one million Jews were slain in the entire tragedy, with hundreds of thousands of others being carried away into slavery.

Verse 24 is the only place in the Bible where the expression "the times of the Gentiles" is found. This is the title for the period of Gentile domination of the holy city—the time when "Jerusalem . . . [is] trodden down of the Gentiles." This epoch had its beginning in 606 B. C. when Nebuchadnezzar first captured the city, and is evidently to continue until the second advent is near. The repossession of the ancient city in June, 1967, by the Israelis is surely a most significant "sign of the times." Someday Jerusalem will at long last find total freedom under its great King.

The message as given by Luke closes with a brief account of what Christ said about events just before and including His return (vv. 25-38).

He Celebrates the Passover with His Disciples and Institutes the Lord's Supper (22:1-38)

His Betrayal Is Plotted by Judas and the Chief Priests (22:1-6)

Since the multitude had so recently extolled the praises of Jesus, the leaders—plotting His death—were afraid to arrest Him openly. When Judas offered to lead them to

Him when He was in some secluded spot, they rejoiced and seized the opportunity. Judas' motive is revealed by the words "They . . . covenanted to give him money." Though outwardly a follower of Christ, he was in actuality a hypocrite (John 6:70; 13:10-11). Love of money was his besetting sin. Already his avarice had led him to theft (John 12:6). Here it was used by Satan to entice him to the sin of betrayal of Christ to His enemies.

He Orders the Upper Room Prepared for the Passover Celebration (22:7-13)

Again Christ displayed His superhuman knowledge in directing the preparations for their eating of the Passover feast. Ancient tradition relates that the place used was John Mark's home, the house Peter went to first when an angel released him from prison (Acts 12:12).

He Eats the Passover with His Disciples (22:14-18)

The brief account in Luke's gospel is all the information we possess concerning the actual Passover celebration that night, though Matthew and Mark give the story of the Lord's Supper that followed. In verse 15 the emphasis is strongly on "*this* passover." This was the Passover before the grand climax, the momentous event for which He had to come to earth. The Passover was fulfilled in the death of Christ—the type in the antitype (v. 16). The cup of verse 17 should not be confused with that which He gave after supper (v. 20).

During the passover feast the cup was circulated four
times, each time having a symbolic value. The last cup
was always the cup of joy. That is the only one to which
Luke refers. There can be no question our Lord partici-
pated in the feast up to this point, up to that last cup, the
cup of joy. This He distributed to them.[1]

He Institutes the Lord's Supper (22:19-20)

Of the gospel writers, only Luke informs us that Jesus
said, "This do in remembrance of me." The chief purpose
of the Lord's Supper is to remind believers of the atoning
death of Christ.

He Foretells His Betrayal (22:21-23)

Let us note . . . that though the wickedness of Judas was
foreknown, and foreseen, and permitted by God in His
infinite wisdom, yet Judas was not the less guilty in God's
sight. God's foreknowledge does not destroy man's responsibility, or justify man in going on still in wickedness,
under the excuse that he cannot help sinning. Nothing
can happen, in heaven or in earth, without God's knowledge and permission. But sinners are always addressed by
God as responsible, and as free agents.[2]

He Teaches the Apostles Concerning Humility and Ser-vice, and Predicts Peter's Denial (22:24-38)

Christ's words to His disciples in verses 35-38 reveal that

[1]G. Campbell Morgan, *The Gospel According to Luke*, pp. 242-43.
[2]J. C. Ryle, *Expository Thoughts on the Gospels, Luke*, p. 402.

conditions in the future were to be quite different from that which they had experienced thus far. Soon they would be out witnessing for Him in the midst of adversity and persecution. They were told to take money and sword with them—the sword not for offense, of course, but for defense.

HE IS BETRAYED IN THE GARDEN OF GETHSEMANE AND TAKEN BEFORE THE COUNCIL (22:39-71)

He Prays in the Garden (22:39-46)

Our Lord was not only the Son of God but also a perfect Man. As a Man He shrank from the awful suffering which He knew was soon to come. But His will was in complete submission to that of the heavenly Father, so that He could pray, "Not my will, but thine, be done." Only Luke tells of the coming of an angel from heaven to strengthen Him (v. 43). The apostles heard the beginning of His prayer but no more, for in weakness they fell asleep (v. 45).

He Is Betrayed by Judas and Taken to the High Priest's House (22:47-54)

Knowing that Jesus often resorted to the garden, Judas anticipated the place where he could find Him, and thus led the enemies to Him. With a hypocritical kiss he identified Christ to the soldiers. Peter, in an attempt to make good his boast that he would stand with the Lord to the end, slashed with his sword at the high priest's servant.

His aim was poor, possibly because of trembling, and only hit the right ear of the man, which was cut off. In mercy, Jesus performed His last miracle of healing by restoring the ear. Even that did not turn them aside from their wicked purpose, for they arrested Him and took Him to the house of the high priest.

He Is Denied by Peter and Condemned by the Sanhedrin (22:55-71)

False witnesses accused Him, but He proclaimed Himself the Son of God and prophesied His future glory. Upon this He was condemned for blasphemy. Meantime Peter, as predicted, denied his Lord.

HE IS CONDEMNED, CRUCIFIED AND BURIED
(23:1-56)

He Is Mocked by Herod and Condemned by Pilate (23:1-25)

While all the gospel writers tell of the appearance of Jesus before Pilate, only Luke speaks of Herod's mocking Him. History calls this man Herod Antipas. His father, Herod the Great, murdered the babes of Bethlehem at the time of Christ's birth. He himself murdered John the Baptist who condemned him for living in adultery with his brother's wife. Jesus applied to him one of the most contemptuous names He ever used for any man—"that fox" (Luke 13:32). Before this time, Herod had desired to meet Jesus (Luke 9:7-9), and had even superstitiously supposed Him to be John risen from the dead (Mark 6:14-16). Hoping to see Christ perform a miracle, he asked Him many questions. When no response was given him by the Lord, he grew angry, showing his spite by mockery and ridicule. Although previously enemies, their common treatment of Jesus brought Herod and Pilate together in friendship that day (v. 12). Theophylact, a twelfth century writer, has said:

> It is a matter of shame to Christians, that while the devil can persuade wicked men to lay aside their enmities, in order to do harm, Christians cannot even keep up friendship in order to do good.[3]

Pilate evidently had some desire to release Jesus, for he knew that He was guilty of no wrongdoing but had been delivered up because of the envy of the rulers. However, he also desired to please the crowd. When he appealed to the people they were moved by the priests to demand that Jesus be crucified. Finally the Roman governor acceded to their wishes, and delivered Him for crucifixion.

He Is Crucified (23:26-49)

After the terrible beating and other torture the Lord was apparently physically exhausted and, therefore, Simon the Cyrenian was impressed into the carrying of the cross. Tradition has it that his two sons (Mark 15:21) later became outstanding leaders in the early church. The

---

[3]Theophylact as cited by *ibid.*, p. 454.

"great company" that followed, lamenting the crime about
to be perpetrated, seemed not to be actual disciples of
Christ, but rather fair-minded and tenderhearted citizens
of Jerusalem who were greatly stirred by such a miscar-
riage of justice.

The Lord urged the daughters of Jerusalem to weep for
themselves instead, as He gave another prediction of the
awful fate soon to befall the city. Though the rulers and
soldiers derided Him, His first words after being placed
on the cross were "Father, forgive them; for they know not
what they do." The Apostle Paul wrote: "Had they known
it, they would not have crucified the Lord of glory" (I
Cor. 2:8). Though they were responsible for their terrible
crime, yet the deed was to some extent mitigated by the
fact that they did not realize who Jesus really was and did
not grasp the full enormity of their awful act. Peter using
similar terms in his sermon on Solomon's porch called on
them to repent (Acts 3:17-19).

Luke alone tells of the penitent thief (v. 42) who, in his
dying moments, rose to great spiritual heights. In asking
the Lord to "remember me when thou comest *in* thy
kingdom" (ASV) he shows a clearer understanding of
Christ's purpose than any of the disciples possessed at that
time.

The answer of Jesus to the thief (v. 43) presents the
strongest assurance anyone could possibly ask. It also shows
the falsity of such errors as purgatory, soul sleep—"the
doctrine that the soul sleeps between death and the

resurrection"[4]—and the insistence that water baptism is necessary to salvation.

He Is Buried (23:50-56)

Joseph of Arimathaea (Mark 15:43; John 19:38) requested the body of Jesus from Pilate and buried it in his new sepulcher nearby. Verse 54 seems to make it clear that the crucifixion took place on Friday.

4Everett F. Harrison (ed.) , *Baker's Dictionary of Theology,* p. 492.

4

The Resurrection and Ascension of the Son of Man

(24:1-53)

He Rises from the Dead and Appears to the Disciples (24:1-49)

THE INTERMENT OF THE BODY of Jesus had been a very hurried matter, since Joseph of Arimathea and Nicodemus (see John 19:38-42) could have had only a very short time to remove His body from the cross and bury it before the Sabbath began at 6 P. M. Indeed, it was only accomplished at all due to the fact that Joseph's tomb was "in the place where he was crucified" (John 19:41). So as day began to dawn on the first day of the week, some of the women came to complete the sad task (v. 10).

But when they arrived at the tomb they found the heavy stone, which they had doubted their ability to move (Mark 16:3), was "rolled away from the sepulcher" (v. 2).

Venturing inside, they found the body gone. Then in their perplexity, suddenly there was the appearance of two beings who looked like men, but had glistening garments. These were angels (see v. 23). In fear the women fell down before these supernatural creatures. The angels spoke words of joyous reproof: "Why seek ye the living among the dead?" (v. 5). These women were reminded that Jesus Himself had promised that He would "rise again." The vision being ended, they rushed back to tell "the eleven," but their testimony was met with unbelief. However, impulsive Peter ran at top speed to check their story at the sepulcher. He, too, found it empty, and finally departed in amazement.

While there are various impressive pieces of evidence to verify the bodily resurrection of our Lord, the two most important proofs are *the empty tomb* and *the postresurrection appearances*. It should be observed that everyone— friends and enemies of Christ alike—acknowledged that though His body was placed in Joseph's new tomb, on the third day that body had totally disappeared and the sepulcher was absolutely empty. The postresurrection appearances complement and explain the empty tomb.

After this, the Lord Jesus appeared to two disciples as they traveled the road to Emmaus (vv. 13-35), a town seven or eight miles from Jerusalem. One of these two was Cleopas. It is not known who the other was, nor why they were journeying to Emmaus.

As they were talking over the monumental events of the last few days, Jesus Himself came up and walked with them. They, however, did not recognize Him, a fact which is plainly stated to have been supernaturally caused (vv. 16, 31). Evidently they, like many others, had been expecting Jesus to bring about a temporal deliverance for Israel. But such hopes had been dashed. The word with which Jesus rebuked them (v. 25) is not the same in the original text as that used in Matthew 5:22. It is not a word of contempt but refers simply to people who do *not* understand what they *ought* to grasp: "O foolish men" (ASV). The Lord Jesus showed that it was *fitting* for the Messiah to suffer and then afterward "enter into his glory." "Ought" (v. 26) is a translation of the same Greek word rendered "behoved" in verse 46.

These Emmaus-bound disciples did not believe "*all* that the prophets have spoken" (v. 25).

> This expression should be carefully noted. The disciples believed *many* things which the prophets had spoken. But they did not believe *all*. They believed the predictions of Messiah's glory, but not of Messiah's sufferings. Christians in modern times too often err in like manner, though in a totally different direction. They believe *all* that the prophets say about Christ's sufferings, but *not all* that they say about Christ coming the second time in glory.[1]

Verse 27 is ample authority for the fact that the Old Testament tells of the coming Saviour from the very beginning.

---

[1] J. C. Ryle, *Expository Thoughts on the Gospels, Luke,* pp. 504-5.

When the disciples were finally allowed to recognize the Lord, He immediately vanished from their sight. This shows that, though His resurrection body was the same physical one in which He died with the marks of His suffering still evident, yet it had passed into a new condition.

Though previously weary from a long walk, everything else was forgotten as the two rushed back to Jerusalem to tell the apostles. "Eleven" is used in verse 33 as a collective term, as Thomas was evidently not present on this occasion. Verse 34 may seem at first sight to contradict Mark 16:13. As to the latter verse,

> this does not imply that none of them believed, but that several, perhaps the greater part, did not believe. When Luke tells us that they said 'the Lord is risen indeed,' we are not to conclude that everyone said this, or even believed it, but only that some believed, and that one of them expressly affirmed it. Such latitude in using pronouns is common in every language.[2]

"As they thus spake," Jesus appeared to the apostles (vv. 36-43). Only Luke records the words spoken by the Lord and the things done by Him mentioned in verses 39-43. This is surely part, at least, of the "many infallible proofs" of the resurrection which Luke later mentions in Acts 1:3.

Though at first glance verses 44-49 appear to be a continuation of what Christ said to the apostles at the time

---

2*Ibid.*, p. 508.

of this opening manifestation, closer attention seems to indicate that such is not the case. They rather represent a general summary of the teaching of the Lord Jesus during the entire forty days of postresurrection ministry.

The apostles evidently considered Christ's resurrection of paramount importance, for they always made it a central theme of their subsequent preaching. Examples of this are to be found in Luke's later book the Acts of the apostles (see, e.g., 2:23-32; 3:15; 10:40-41; 13:29-31; 17:31; 26:8, 22-23). The Lord Jesus repeatedly foretold this great occurrence (e.g., Luke 9:22). If He was right even about such a stupendous thing as this, surely we can trust all of His claims: that He is the unique Son of God (Luke 10:22; 22:70); that salvation is to be found through His atoning death (Luke 19:10; 22:19-20); that all His teaching is absolute truth which will never "pass away" (Luke 21:33).

He Ascends to Heaven and the Disciples Return to Jerusalem (24:50-53)

Luke's account of the ascension is quite brief. However, he had full information on the subject, which material he presents later in the first chapter of his Acts of the apostles. The present writing may have been made short deliberately with the idea of future amplification.

In the closing scene, the Lord Jesus Christ blessed the disciples, then ascended to heaven. There, Luke tells us later, He seated Himself at the place of closest access to the Father (Acts 2:33; 7:55-56). There He serves as our great

High Priest (Heb. 4:14). This is really the central theme of the epistle to the Hebrews. Indeed, it has been the opinion of some authorities, since early days in church history, that Luke himself was the writer of that epistle.[3] The disciples worshiped Him and with joy returned to Jerusalem to wait there as He had commanded. The statement that they "were *continually* in the temple" should not be understood as meaning that they spent twenty-four hours a day in that place, but rather that daily and frequently they worshiped in the house of God. This ending to the third gospel may seem a bit abrupt, but it appears evident that Luke contemplated writing an additional book which would give more complete information not only about the ascension but also the subsequent actions of the apostles. Soon the Holy Spirit would come and "repentance and remission of sins" would indeed "be preached in his name among all nations" (Luke 24:47). This witness still goes on and will continue to do so until He comes again (Acts 1:8-11).

---

[3]*Pulpit Commentary*, **XXI**, xii.

Bibliography

Erdman, Charles R. *The Gospel of Luke, An Exposition.* Philadelphia: Westminster, 1942.

Harrison, Everett F. (ed.). *Baker's Dictionary of Theology.* Grand Rapids: Baker, 1960.

The International Standard Bible Encyclopaedia. Grand Rapids: Eerdmans, 1949.

Ironside, H. A. *Addresses on Luke.* New York: Loizeaux, 1946.

———. *Expository Notes on the Gospel of Mark.* New York: Loizeaux, 1952.

Jamieson, Robert; Fausset, A. R.; and Brown, David. *A Commentary on the Old and New Testaments.* Vol. V. Grand Rapids: Eerdmans, 1948.

Jukes, Andrew. *Four Views of Christ.* Grand Rapids: Kregel, 1966.

Kelly, William. *Exposition of the Gospel of Luke.* London: Holness, 1914.

Meyer, F. B. *Peter: Fisherman, Disciple, Apostle.* Grand Rapids: Zondervan, 1950.

Morgan, G. Campbell. *The Gospel According to Luke.* New York: Revell, 1932.

———. *The Gospel According to Matthew.* New York: Revell, 1949.

———. *The Parables and Metaphors of Our Lord.* New York: Revell, 1943.

Pulpit Commentary. Vol. XVI: Mark and Luke. Grand Rapids: Eerdmans, 1950.

Ryle, J. C. *Expository Thoughts on the Gospels, Luke.* Grand Rapids: Zondervan, n.d.

Scofield, C. I. *The Scofield Reference Bible.* New York: Oxford, 1945.

Simpson, E. K. and Bruce, F. F. *The New International Commentary on the New Testament: Ephesians and Colossians.* Grand Rapids: Eerdmans, 1957.

Thomas, W. H. Griffith. *Outline Studies in the Gospel of Luke.* Grand Rapids: Eerdmans, 1950.

Thompson, D. A. *Jerusalem and the Temples in Bible History and Prophecy.* London: Sovereign Grace, n.d.

Trench, R. C. *Synonyms of the New Testament.* Grand Rapids: Eerdmans, 1948.

Vine, W. E. *An Expository Dictionary of New Testament Words.* Westwood, N.J.: Revell, 1948.